# PAY OFF YOUR
# MORTGAGE
# IN 2 YEARS

Thanks to Lucy Clemence, Julie Garnett, Andrew Miles,
Pip, George and William

*'Some debts are fun when
you are acquiring them,
but none are fun when
you set about retiring them.'*
Ogden Nash, US poet (1902–71)

*'There are but two ways
of paying debt:
increase of industry in
raising income, increase
of thrift in laying out.'*
Thomas Carlyle, Scottish essayist (1795–1881)

# PAY OFF YOUR MORTGAGE IN 2 YEARS

Graham Hooper

BOOKS

This book is published to accompany the television series *Pay Off Your Mortgage in 2 Years*, produced by BBC Birmingham and broadcast on BBC2 in 2006. Executive producer: Emma Willis

Published by BBC Books, BBC Worldwide Ltd,
Woodlands, 80 Wood Lane,
London W12 0TT

First published in 2006
Reprinted 2006
Copyright © Graham Hooper 2006
The moral right of the author has been asserted.

ISBN 0 563 52284 4

Commissioning editor: Nicky Ross
Project editor: Laura Nickoll
Copy-editors: Patricia Burgess and Helena Caldon
Designer: Bobby Birchall at DW Design
Production controller: Kenneth McKay

Set in Glypha and Frutiger
Printed and bound in Great Britain by CPI Bath

For more information about this and other BBC books, please call 08700 777 001 or visit our website at www.bbcshop.co.uk

# Contents

# Foreword

**Today a mortgage** usually means a huge financial liability that will generate significant interest and will require 25 years of due care and attention – 25 long years! This huge debt burden casts a shadow over most of our working lives – we need to change our attitudes towards it now and do all we can to rid ourselves of the load as soon as possible.

Being British, we see our homes as our castles and consequently, for most of us, the offer of a mortgage on the house of our dreams is a cause for celebration. This should not be the case: a mortgage is probably the biggest, most expensive loan you will ever take on and must not be a cause for celebration – it is really a cause for despair!

A recent survey found that the one thing that would most change our lives for the better is paying off our mortgage. Now just hold on there; don't laugh and say, 'If only'. It can be achieved and, make no mistake, it can be achieved by real people like you and me. *Pay Off Your Mortgage in 2 Years* will show you how and how not to attempt it.

The television series proves how ordinary people can achieve extraordinary results just by sheer determination and discipline and without high finance or complex algorithms. To accompany this series, Graham Hooper has crafted an excellent and easy-to-read guide to paying off your mortgage early.

In contrast to the many impenetrable reference books on personal finance that are available, Graham has illustrated his advice using real-life case studies that can be followed in the TV series. In the process, he has demystified the mortgage maze and has explained in simple language how to plot a path to freedom. By the time you have finished this book you will definitely want to explore the possibility of paying off your mortgage early. And when you have agreed that you have absolutely nothing to lose and all to gain, this book will stay by your side through one of the most profitable and exciting journeys you will ever make.

All the contributors to the TV series have bravely taken the first step on the ladder to financial independence. There are no guarantees or easy routes and one size does not fit all. The first step is to understand your inherent strengths and play to them. Set yourself challenges that will help you to explore what you are good at, and elicit advice on the things that you find difficult or dull. Working within your capabilities makes a process enjoyable, unconditionally worthwhile and something to look forward to.

This might be the biggest financial decision you have to consider, but it is also the most obvious and might be the best one you ever make. Just ask yourself the simple question: what have you got to lose?

**René Carayol**

*René Carayol, presenter of the Pay Off Your Mortgage in 2 Years series, is one of the UK's few authentic business gurus. Having worked for the likes of Marks and Spencer, been on the board of Pepsi UK, and spent three years as a non-executive director of the Inland Revenue, when it comes to business he knows what he is talking about.*

*René has served as advisor to the The Prime Minister's Delivery Unit and is also visiting professor at CASS Business School. An author and regular voice on BBC Radio, he has also conducted onstage interviews with Bill Clinton, Mikhail Gorbachev and Madeleine Albright, all in the same day at the Leaders in London Conference 2005! He spends his time working with organizations and individuals from the private and public sector, as a coach, a mentor and a leader.*

*René was awarded an MBE in 2004 for outstanding service to the business community.*

# Introduction

**With over £1 trillion** worth of borrowings, UK consumers are more heavily in debt now than they have ever been, and that includes you and me – real people. This surging debt has been used to buy bigger and better houses, second properties and consumer goods, such as cars, washing machines and mobile phones. Rampant consumerism on the back of rampant debt has kept the stock market ticking along and probably kept Tony Blair in power, but one day the chickens will come home to roost.

This book is about an experiment in regaining financial control. It focuses on six couples and two individuals with various skills, interests and determination to see if, through efficient budgeting and building businesses, they can save and make enough money to pay off mortgages ranging from £50,000 to £233,000 within two years. In the process of telling you about the experiences of these guinea pigs, the book aims to leave you fully informed about mortgages and other forms of debt so that you too can set about making enough money to pay off your own mortgage early.

Alongside guidelines for success are warnings about financial traps and pitfalls. There is a lot to take into account, but the benefits are huge. Not only can you repay the capital element of your mortgage, but the interest as well. This could have a massive effect on your lifetime earnings. Sean and Anne-Marie, for example, have a mortgage of £84,920, and the interest on that mortgage over the term comes to a whopping £71,621, making a total mortgage debt of £156,541. If they pay off their mortgage early, they could have that hefty sum to open up a whole range of new and exciting opportunities – work fewer hours, go on more and better holidays, help the children out financially, retire in comfort, climb more mountains, eat more ice cream – whatever they want.

This is the real point of paying off a mortgage early: it's not just about money – it's about having the freedom to make choices in life. Getting rid of that financial ball and chain probably won't be easy, but it's definitely worthwhile – and if you don't do it now, when will you?

The original aim with the contributors was to see if they could pay off their mortgages within two years. This time frame won't suit everyone, and it might not suit you, but even if you pay off only half your mortgage in two years you'll be a lot better off than doing nothing. Of course, you'll have to think about how you are going to achieve this, and I'll be giving you lots of ideas to help you along. I'll also be explaining in simple terms why paying off your mortgage is so worthwhile: there's nothing to lose, and so much to gain. Just imagine how good you'll feel to have lost such a big chunk of your financial burden.

Good luck if you decide to go for it, and do let us know how you get on.

Best wishes

**Graham Hooper**

*Graham Hooper was born in Cornwall in 1959. He graduated from Greenwich University with a first class honours degree in business studies and a distinction in HND business studies in 1983. Following that, he helped grow Chase de Vere to a value of £132 million, at which point it was sold to the Bank of Ireland. He was business development director with Bradford & Bingley as well as working with the BBC as a financial pundit and commentator and a business consultant to M&G, Standard Life, Midas Capital Partners, Novartis, Keydata and Cavendish Grant.*

*He is currently marketing director for AWD Chase de Vere, the largest independent financial advisers in the UK and Europe.*

# Meet the Contributors

**Six couples and two individuals** were recruited to participate in a two-year experiment, the object being to see if they could achieve what we would all like to do – pay off the mortgage early and do something more interesting with the money. Their reasons for doing so are as various as the people themselves. I have drawn up the following profiles so that you can learn a bit about them and see how I initially rated their chances of success. Perhaps you can adapt their experiences to your own situation and – most importantly – learn from their mistakes.

## Simon and Debbie Binner

Simon (46) and Debbie (40) live on the outskirts of London with their three children. Simon works in information technology and Debbie works in PR for the National Health Service. They have a mortgage of £233,000.

Simon and Debbie

The Binners are very different from the other contributors. For a start, they have a whacking great mortgage and a lifestyle to match their six-figure income. Both are very successful at their chosen careers, and are reaping the financial rewards of years of hard work and commitment.

Despite all the trappings of success, this apparently 'golden couple' believe that they are working hard to maintain a lifestyle that they do not really enjoy. Time is at a premium and they feel trapped by their success. When discussing their situation, they use telling phrases, such as 'stuck in a rut' and 'on a treadmill'.

By most people's standards, a lifestyle that includes personal yoga tuition at home, private schools for the children, gym membership, a house worth almost £1 million, two cars, great holidays and eating out regularly is something to be envied. Debbie and Simon, though, are pretty downbeat about it.

Debbie would like to leave her job within the NHS and set up her own business doing some kind of media or PR training, probably in the corporate field. She is also interested in becoming a yoga, body control or Pilates teacher. There's no doubt that she is very driven to create something for herself, but leaving a reasonably well-paid and secure job to set up a brand-new business with no guarantee of success is a very big step. A drop in income may be just too unpalatable given her lifestyle.

While the Binners' mortgage is big – £233,000 – they have no other debts, and their substantial income is enough to support a mortgage of this size. They also have tons of equity in their house – probably over £500,000 – and hefty savings in excess of £100,000. So if all else fails, and they do jump off their self-inflicted treadmill, they can always sell their house and downsize to a more manageable mortgage – or not have one at all.

## Money-making ideas

The couple's main idea is to pay off the mortgage by using the income from Debbie's new business, but that will take time to materialize. Debbie also wants to buy an investment property somewhere in Europe. Given the other demands on her time, I think this is a wild card, and I can't see it coming to fruition.

One idea for Simon to make more money is to renegotiate his sales territory with his employer so that it includes a more lucrative area. He's good at his job, so this wouldn't be a risk to either side. As part of his remuneration is commission-based, the uplift in his earnings could be significant, but it's impossible to quantify the gain at this stage.

Simon also wants to give private maths tuition to schoolchildren at £65 per session three times a week. I feel that both the price for the tuition and the number of sessions are over-optimistic, especially as Simon has a full-time job that might become even more onerous if his sales territory increases.

There are many uncertainties around the Binners' ideas for making money, so it is essential to get the budgeting right. For people like Simon and Debbie, used to a lavish lifestyle, this won't be easy. After tax, their monthly income is very healthy – over £6,000. Fixed monthly costs, including school fees, gas, electricity, water, council tax and Simon's pension, come to £2,812 per month. Now this is where it gets interesting. On top of that, they spend a colossal £5,314, on average, month in month out.

## Budgeting

The good news from a budgeting perspective is that there is plenty of scope for improvement and huge savings to be harvested. In the end, we gave them a budget of £346 per week (£1,500 per month). If they keep to it, they can save around £4,300 per month or an incredible £103,200 over the course of the two-year experiment – almost half of their £233,000 mortgage. Personally, I reckon they will do well to save half that amount – £50,000. What this illustrates is that if you don't save money from budgeting, you have to make it up on the business ideas side of the equation, and that can be far more difficult and challenging.

There are several risks with the Binners. First, I just don't believe that they will be able to stick to their budget, even with total mortgage and interest savings of almost £500,000 at stake. Second, their business ideas will take time to come to fruition, yet time is one thing they lack.

While Simon and Debbie say they want to change their life, I feel they are just too comfortable where they are and how they live and can't help wondering whether they're really willing to give it up. They'll give it a go, but are probably in the most difficult position of all the contributors. They can definitely pay off their mortgage early, but their current lifestyle is going to get in the way and will, I believe, stop them from doing the things they really need to do in order to get there.

## RENÉ'S SUMMARY

Debbie and Simon are adamant that they don't want to sacrifice their comfortable lifestyle in any way, and would rather generate more money through business ventures. They are willing to work hard in order to make the £233,000 needed to clear the mortgage, and they are both confident that it can be done.

## Sean and Anne-Marie Casey-Poole

Sean and Anne-Marie are in their 30s and live in Coventry. Anne-Marie works as a marketing assistant for a high street bank and Sean is an account manager for a different bank. They have two children and an £85,000 mortgage.

Neither Sean nor Anne-Marie were particularly happy in their jobs. They find their real enjoyment in outside interests. Anne-Marie was once a karaoke hostess, while Sean is a comedy hypnotist and performs in pubs and clubs up and down the country.

With Sean now approaching 40, they feel they need to pay serious consideration to their future and take steps to improve their financial security. Paying off their mortgage will be a colossal step forward.

Considering that they both work in banks, this couple's finances are in not in great shape. The mortgage they have is actually only part of their problem. They have another £16,000 in consolidation loans, which they took out to clear their credit card debt. On top of this they are paying £5,000 on a car loan, £1,500 on three separate overdrafts and £1,000 on a store card. Added to that, their monthly outgoings exceed their monthly income by a massive £1,537.

There are two issues that need urgent atttention: they over-spend regularly and they don't really discuss what's going on with their finances.

### Money-making ideas

Anne-Marie would be far happier working for the bank on a part-time basis and spending the rest of her time running weight-loss classes. She recently lost 7 stone in ten months, reducing from a size 22 to a size 8, and is now evangelical about helping others to achieve similar results. She has the enthusiasm to spread the word, but good ideas depend on far more than idealism. I reckon she will be lucky if the classes contribute £10,000 over the two-year period (see her figures on page 168-169).

Bearing in mind that Anne-Marie has a full-time job and her income is significant to the family, I can only see the weight-loss classes starting as evening events, progressing to full time if they are successful. Anne-Marie is also keen to use her secretarial skills on a freelance basis, but I doubt she will have the time. What about her karaoke ability? Well, she has a great voice and could make around £100 per night singing, but she doesn't like doing it.

Sean's ideas revolve around his interest in comedy hypnosis and neuro-linguistic programming (NLP). NLP offers methods of understanding how we think, behave and change. It aims to make people adaptable in a changing environment. He has experience in the entertainment world and isn't one of those starry-eyed people bent on success at all costs. If he does only three shows a week at £150 per show for 40 weeks a year, he's looking at an annual income of £18,000. If two of those shows were at weekends, he could charge £350 a time, which would increase his annual income to £34,000. If he could get one NLP job a week at £1,000 over 50 weeks, Sean would be looking at £50,000 annual income. He could even supplement this income by selling add-ons, such as slimming books, CDs and tapes to go with Anne-Marie's slimming classes. He could also produce some as aids to giving up smoking and handling stress. Perhaps we could introduce Sean to Mary Holleyman (see page 20), who's also in the stress-busting business. Joined-up thinking can often be the catalyst that makes a plan come to fruition.

## Budgeting

Given their debts and chronic overspending, Sean and Anne-Marie have to be reined in. We gave them a budget of £155 per week (£620 per month), and they are making huge efforts to live within it. In the first four months of the experiment, they were overspending their budget by around £85 per week, although some of this money was being spent to develop new business ventures. This was an outstanding effort given where they started from, but far short of where they needed to get to. A lot therefore depends on their business ideas.

Sean's hypnosis will have to deliver the goods to get close to the target. My worry is that he is more in love with the *idea* of this radical career shift than with the reality. How will he get to all the extra shows he plans to do? How will he feel about being away from the family? He will need a lot of energy, and additional help with marketing to make a success of things. However, even if Sean is only a quarter as successful as he hopes, it could be enough to set the couple on the road to paying off their mortgage early.

Although I wonder if the couple will have sufficient discipline to see things through and cope with difficulties, they are very willing to give it a go. I think they secretly hope that the TV exposure will help launch Sean's entertainment career and give them a much-needed boost. Their positive attitude gives me hope for their future.

### RENÉ'S SUMMARY

**Sean seems to be an obvious entrepreneur while Anne-Marie seems to be an obvious manager – but I could be wrong. I know what Anne-Marie's dream is, but I don't know what Sean's is and neither does he. If he doesn't find out soon, he will never pay off his mortgage in two years.**

## Julie Edosa

Julie is in her late 40s, but doesn't look it. She lives in Bristol, where she works as a management accountant, and has two children in their 20s, and a mortgage of £75,000.

I liked Julie from the moment I met her. She is a warm, generous and outgoing person, who talks at top speed and seems to know her own mind. According to her daughters, she likes a good party, too. I believe her desire to pay off her mortgage early is genuine, but I wonder if she can channel her fun-loving energy into a money-making enterprise.

Julie lives alone, but has a relatively new partner who lives about 190 km (120 miles) away. He and her two grown-up children are supportive of her attempt to pay off the mortgage. She would like to be free of this financial burden because she wants to set up her own business at some point in the future. She plans to rent out some rooms in her house (something she intended to do before the series came up), but progress on the final decoration is very slow because she is a perfectionist and wants everything done just so.

Julie's big weakness is that she just can't stop buying treats for herself, her family and her friends. In fact, 'treats' really doesn't tell the whole story. At the time I met her she had just bought herself a coat costing £650. She also likes good food and wine, so I'm sure she will find it difficult to cut back on her favourite luxury – champagne.

### Money-making ideas

She needs to occupy her time so that she doesn't have the opportunities to go out and spend, spend, spend. While she has a few ideas for making money, I feel she will need a lot of help to come up with more if she is going to be able to pay off her mortgage. Given her background in business, she works well to deadlines, so I wondered if organizing corporate events, which involve a series of deadlines, might be something she could turn her hand to. A lump sum at the end of a long job might suit her better than receiving frequent small sums from a series of short-term jobs.

As well as enjoying regular treats and good wine and food, Julie also likes to eat out, often travels the long distance to see her partner and spends about £1,600 on holidays every year. To fund all this she has built up a debt on her credit cards of around £15,000. This is a bad situation for anyone, but she really should know better.

Helping Julie to pay off her mortgage will not be easy. She has to stop buying treats, firm up her vague ideas and apply her business head to her own personal circumstances. For someone who finds it hard to exert financial self-discipline, this is a tall order.

Of the few money-making ideas Julie has, the one she likes best (because it's within her comfort zone) is to remortgage her house to release some equity, then buy a property abroad to develop and rent out or sell. This idea concerns me because of the risk involved in trying to turn a substantial profit within two years. That's really not long enough to be certain of the return.

Another plan is to sell cosmetics on the Internet, but she knows little about the intricacies of the cosmetics market and online selling. She also talks of setting up a weekly stall at Bristol Market to sell sporting goods. While relatively low risk, there are limits to how much one stall can sell, and again I feel this plan lacks substance. The best bet is her idea of letting out rooms in her house. It utilizes one of her latent assets and is relatively low maintenance, but although it is a low-maintenance option, this alone will not pay off her mortgage early.

Commitment will be a key factor in Julie's success. She refuses to let her day job suffer while she attempts to become an entrepreneur;

she also wants to see her grown-up daughters regularly and to spend every other weekend with her boyfriend, who lives a long way from Bristol. While she is keen to pay off her mortgage, I don't think she fully appreciates the sacrifices she will have to make in order to do so.

## Budgeting

Now you might think that Julie, being an accountant, would have the business of budgeting well under control. However, she regularly overspends by £456 per month, but the real shock to me is the amount of monthly interest she is paying on credit and charge cards – a whopping £324 a month.

As with many of the contributors, there is a risk that Julie will spend more time dreaming than doing. This would be bad news because a week lost here and there will make her numbers difficult to achieve. Another risk is that her enthusiasm will lead her to take on more projects than she can comfortably manage with a full-time job. Overstretching is never a good idea.

However, Julie is a driven woman. Paying off her mortgage is something that she really wants to do – with or without the help of the TV series. Sometimes she loses focus, so she must learn that no one can afford to tick over for long when turning a marathon into a sprint. We need to drive her towards finding a genuine money-making idea. Only then will she really make inroads into paying off her mortgage. I'm confident she can do it – the only question is when.

### RENÉ'S SUMMARY

Julie is very hardworking between the hours of 9 and 5.30, and she follows a clear process that never requires her to be creative. She's not brilliant at business initiatives. To pay off a mortgage in two years requires more than just hard work. Julie will have to be more creative and will have to identify some sort of business initiative in order to succeed.

## Arthur and Mary Holleyman

Arthur and Mary are in their 50s and live in Essex. Arthur is a print technology engineer and Mary is an aromatherapist and reiki healer. They have three mortgages totalling £139,500: one mort-

gage on their own house for £8,300 (including a home improvement loan); another on Mary's parents' house, which they also own, for £34,200; and one on a property in El Gouna, Egypt, which will rise to £97,000 by the end of 2006. The El Gouna loan is unusual in that they have to pay off £12,500 every three months, for which they utilize a £100,000 facility secured against their own home. To complicate things further, the staged £12,500 payments need to be paid in US dollars, so there's a further risk in moving their money from sterling to dollars, and a cost of around 2% for the currency transaction. The total value of the three mortgaged properties is £427,000.

Arthur is considering retiring in about two years' time, so trying to pay off the mortgages early is a big issue for him and Mary. Having been shown what they have been spending over the years, Mary and Arthur are appalled at the amount of money they feel they have squandered rather than putting it towards the single most important financial issue in their lives – paying off the mortgages.

So where has the money been going? Mary and Arthur have a relatively healthy monthly net income which breaks down as follows:

| | |
|---|---|
| Mary's business | £700 |
| Arthur's salary | £2,308 |
| **Total:** | **£3,008** |

The couple have been earning around £50,000 per annum before tax and like their treats. For their ruby wedding anniversary they went to Egypt on holiday and threw a huge party to celebrate with their friends. They are also generous: they pay for their parents to go on holidays, and would love to give financial help to their children.

## Money-making ideas

When I first talked to them, they had very few viable ideas for creating a business that could make a serious dent in their mortgages. Mary had once run a cleaning company but became nervous when her accountant advised her to expand it, and decided to give it up. Having put the cleaning company on hold, Mary started an aromatherapy and massage business. She won a lucrative contract with the nearby TNT offices to treat employees in situ, and this was a resounding success from everyone's point of view. In fact, Mary ended up employing other aromatherapists to satisfy the demand, but she was stopped in her tracks by the Inland Revenue, who suggested that her services were a 'benefit in kind' and that TNT might be obliged to tax its employees for the treatments. Instead of dealing with this glitch, Mary allowed the business to wind down. This was one area she could try to get going again – it had not completely wound down, so it just needed a kick-start.

Luckily, she found another business idea while attending a jewellery party – sourcing jewellery from the Far East and importing it to sell in the UK. She and a friend decided to join forces and sell Candy Crystal Jewellery at parties, in retail outlets and on the Internet. This offered a great opportunity for high profit margins.

## Budgeting

Budgeting is a crucial issue for Arthur and Mary. They regularly overspend by £534 per month, and have other debts totalling £19,350. We gave them a budget of £503 per month, and so far they are managing to stick to it.

The biggest risk with the couple is that they don't have the necessary skill sets to fully exploit their business opportunities and could lack organization. But they are willing to give it their all – Mary especially has bucketloads of energy and enthusiasm. We need to make sure that she sticks to one or two ideas and channels her energy appropriately into them. Arthur's position will hopefully be as the organizer, preventing Mary from being diverted from the task ahead. They will need to remain focused.

Another risk is that, in the context of paying off the mortgage early, this was a big idea that would need her full-time commitment, allowing little time to focus on the other ideas.

I believe that rigid budgeting combined with Mary's jewellery venture and reviving the aromatherapy business will give the couple a good chance of paying off their mortgage in two years. My worry is that Mary won't have the energy to cope with restarting one business and co-running another. These factors will probably make the difference between success and failure.

### RENÉ'S SUMMARY
**Arthur and Mary are a great couple – a rock-solid unit, full of ideas and with a good reason to want to pay off their mortgages. I'm as confident as it is possible to be that they can pay it off, and in the two-year time frame.**

## Duncan Hume

Duncan, aged 32, lives in London and is a professional ballet dancer. He has a mortgage of £53,000.

Gifted, good-looking and very fit, Duncan has a lot going for him. He is able to pursue a career that he adores and his parents are very supportive, but money slips through his hands like sand: if he earns it, he spends it. The more he earns, the more treats he gives himself. He never knows what he's earned or where it goes. So he has at least two problems: little notion of budgeting and no concept of saving.

It took a long time to tease out the root cause of Duncan's parlous financial state, but we got there eventually. It seems that he has been receiving financial support from his parents – not just a little here and there, but to the tune of thousands of pounds a year. We had to come up with some ideas, and quickly, to put an end to Duncan's dependence on outside help.

### Money-making ideas

He was full of ideas, from the first time I met him, and his schemes ranged far and wide. He wants to set up regular urban ballet classes in London, while also going to Japan to perform with a ballet troupe. (He didn't seem to register that doing both might be a problem from a geographical point of view.) He also wants to establish his own dance troupe and build up his modelling work. Another idea is property renovation – the sort of thing half the world is currently up to. He's also thought about selling his assets, taking in a lodger, temping in offices, cooking for dinner parties and making cakes to sell in

London's Borough Market. At first I thought, 'great – lots of ideas', but that was part of Duncan's problem – they were only ideas: he hadn't seriously thought them through, worked out how he was going to implement them or even calculated the income they could realistically generate.

It was pretty clear that he doesn't have one big idea that we could go to war with and make him his £53,000. He's a butterfly by nature and he will never concentrate for two years on one project. Fortunately, I feel that Duncan can cope with a number of projects, but they will really have to appeal to him in order to keep him interested and committed. He knows nothing about sales or marketing, so he must get appropriate help and learn to cope with pressure.

Making money from teaching dancing is tough, and I feel that Duncan will not be able to cope with the administration. In one conversation with him I asked what happens if he feels he is having an 'off' day, expecting an answer such as, 'I dance my way through it'. Oh, no. Duncan's solution is to 'make a cup of tea, go to bed and watch *Countdown* until I feel better'. This speaks volumes. We aren't dealing with a hugely driven human being here – and if he doesn't commit to his ideas, we'll be struggling from day one.

## Budgeting

Part of Duncan's problem is that he never knows where he is with money. The numbers he originally provided just didn't add up. When I first went through his income and expenditure, it looked as if he was overspending by several thousands of pounds every year, yet his overdraft was relatively small and constant. After a little probing, he came clean. His parents were bailing him out every month – and had been for years. This gave a huge insight into why Duncan behaves the way he does. Mum and Dad fund his lifestyle and he can be as relaxed about income, expenditure and mortgage as he wants to be.

It's virtually impossible to get Duncan to commit to a budget, but we set him a weekly target of roughly £70 (£305 per month) to cover food, entertainment and ballet classes. His total monthly budget was therefore £681 + £305 = £986. Tight but fair, I thought. So far, Duncan is nowhere near keeping to this target – not even close. He struggles with self-discipline and has never had to make sacrifices. In 2004 he was given approximately £10,000 by his parents and another £7,000 by his generous grandmother.

Although Duncan keeps talking about changing his life in order to pay off his mortgage, staying committed to that goal is going to be a huge challenge for him. Time will tell what he's made of, but I don't have high hopes of his success.

### RENÉ'S SUMMARY

Duncan has proved himself before, by becoming a ballet dancer at the age of 22. However, his parents have been in the background pulling the levers for nearly everything else he has achieved thus far. This time it's going to have to be different. He's got to do it on his own ... and I'm going to be there to ensure that he does.

## Paddy and Mandy MacVean

Paddy and Mandy are in their mid-40s and live in Guildford. Paddy is a self-employed builder and decorator and Mandy is a religious education teacher. They have three school-age children and a £51,000 mortgage.

Paddy and Mandy

Family is paramount to Paddy and Mandy, and money is not a significant problem, but with few savings and a negligible pension for Paddy, they know they must take serious steps to make themselves more financially secure. They paid £305,000 for their house, which is now worth around £450,000, and have a facility to increase their mortgage to £140,000.

Paying off their mortgage early is something Paddy really wants to do, but he doesn't want their children to suffer in the process.

Paddy and Mandy enjoy a healthy income of over £40,000 a year, which breaks down as follows:

| | |
|---|---|
| Paddy | £1,167 |
| Mandy | £2,000 |
| Child Benefit | £154 |
| Child Tax Credit | £40 |
| **Total per month:** | **£3,361** |

Their fixed monthly costs of mortgage, gas, electricity and insurance come to £1,059 per month, but what really bumps up their outgoings is regular credit card payments of £1,050 per month. As with many people, their expenditure seems to rise to meet income and they regularly overspend by about £600 each month. This gives a total monthly expenditure of £3,939. Budgeting is going to be important for this family.

## Money-making ideas

The couple have no shortage of ideas for making extra money – from using Paddy's expertise in building, to starting a dog-walking service, throwing children's parties, offering respite fostering and making videos of children at school to sell to their parents. This last idea concerned me because, good as Paddy's intentions are, he is smack into child protection territory. He will need to seek out specialist advice and follow proper procedures.

The best bet by far is to use Paddy's skills in the property area. By utilizing the 'spare' mortgage facility of up to £89,000, they could buy a property – probably abroad – refurbish it and sell it on for a profit. If they do this twice in the two years and make £20,000 each time, they could make £40,000 – a huge dent in the £51,000 needed. If they decide on this strategy, they must plan it out as soon as possible and get on with it quickly. Two years sounds a long time, but finding the property, purchasing it, planning the works and budgeting for the refurbishment can easily take months before any hammering and sawing actually starts.

However, the couple will also need to implement their other ideas as it is unlikely that they can reach their goal on Paddy's skills alone. The figures that could be raised from other activities work out as follows:

| | | |
|---|---|---|
| **Dog walking** | once a week at £10 a time = £500 p.a. x 2 years = | £1,000 |
| **Lodger from the local school** | £185 per week x 12 weeks = £2,220 x 2 years = | £4,440 |
| **Mandy marking exams** | £1,000 p.a. x 2 years = | £2,000 |
| **Children's parties** | £15 per child x 10 children = £150 x 6 times p.a. = £900 x 2 years = | £1,800 |

| | | |
|---|---|---:|
| **Respite fostering** | £75 per day x 1 day per month x 12 months = | |
| | £900 x 2 years = | £1,800 |
| **Utilize current savings** | £150 per month x 24 months = | £3,600 |
| **Stop giving to charity** | £100 per month x 24 months = | £2,400 |

(The donations can be reinstated at a higher level after they've paid off their mortgage.)

**TOTAL: £17,040**

The total benefit from all this would be £59,920, which means that the whole mortgage would be paid off in two years, leaving around £9,000 contingency money.

## Budgeting
After going through their monthly expenditure, they found they could also save a relatively painless £816 per month just by cutting back slightly.

| | |
|---|---|
| Cancelled standing orders and direct debits for magazines, pocket money and ISA contributions | £221 |
| Phone bill | £18 |
| Food | £300 |
| Clothes | £75 |
| Bank charges | £60 |
| DIY | £80 |
| Furniture | £62 |
| **Total monthly saving:** | **£816** |

Over 24 months this amounts to £19,604 – not far off half their £56,709 mortgage (taking into account redemption fees). By giving up holidays and other treats, they could halve their mortgage in two years just by efficient budgeting. That's a number worth fighting for.

So far as the property venture is concerned, a big risk involves Paddy: what if he doesn't get on quickly enough with finding the property, buying it and refurbishing it? He's already mentioned the possibility of employing someone. To me this seemed potentially disastrous as his property plan relies on big profits. Employing the wrong person might kill it. Also, how would he feel about living away from the family on his own? It's easy to commit at the 'ideas' stage, but you have to think through all the implications for your life as well as your finances.

My concern about Paddy and Mandy is that the involvement of TV and all that it entails might be a distraction for them.

They are good people with sound ideas, but they are very comfortable where they are within the family unit and community. Do they really have the motivation over two years to carry this off? I have my doubts.

## RENÉ'S SUMMARY

Paddy and Mandy are one of the most selfless couples I've ever met. The reason behind their desire to pay off their mortgage is to get their children through college. But they lack a ruthless streak and without it I'm not sure that they will achieve this, but they will make a difference.

## Dan Harding and Lucy Aldridge

Dan and Lucy are in their early 30s and live in Cornwall with their two children. They have a mortgage of £105,000.

Dan and Lucy

Money has never featured largely in this couple's life. They live on the outskirts of St Ives amid beautiful natural surroundings and are keen surfers. In fact, the only thing they love more than the sea is each other. As delightful as Dan and Lucy are, their attitude towards money is going to cause them real problems in the future. But trying to get them to focus on something they are really not interested in is an immense challenge.

Dan does what I call 'creative engineering', making works of art and domestic items from found objects. For example, he makes wood-burning stoves from gas bottles, saucepans and bits of scrap metal, and turns old fire extinguishers into coal scuttles. His creations are both beautiful and useful.

Lucy is a yoga teacher and simply wants to be the best in the world. When not working, she and Dan, together with their two sons, spend much of their time surfing. They live a happy-go-lucky life, but the lack of financial security is a bit scary.

In terms of outgoings, Dan and Lucy overspend by £321.21 a month. They also make two payments on bank and credit card charges – £90 per month. This is an area to attack straight away. If we can knock these down, we could save them £1,080 a year.

### Money-making ideas

Dan has lots of ideas for making more money, but I feel they are unrealistic for two reasons: first, there are too many of them, and second, most of them are too labour-intensive – he just won't have enough time to fulfil them. For example, his Volkswagen-camshaft candlesticks look great – truly inventive and innovative – but it is very difficult and time consuming to source the parts, and the market for them is probably tiny. Standing about 60 cm (2 ft) tall and weighing 9 kg (20 lb), they're unlikely to be found sitting on the dining tables of middle England. His wood-burning stoves not only look fantastic, but work very well too. Their slight quirkiness makes them a real talking point. At the moment he is selling them too cheaply – at around £600 a time. To me, they look like at least £1,000 of anyone's money. Dan underestimates and undervalues both his ability and his time. We toyed with a few ideas, but he dismissed them as too expensive. Don't you wish more people could be like him?

Lucy's aim is to raise her profile as a yoga teacher, increase her classes and start teaching a new kind of yoga specifically for surfers. However, I'm not sure that St Ives is the best place to fulfil her ambition of becoming the 'best yoga teacher in the world'. She would need to up her qualifications quickly to give her credibility and status. Then there is the commercial angle to consider. She would need to be teaching regularly, as well as developing ideas to run in parallel with her core business. This means DVDs, books, yoga equipment and, possibly, aromatherapy. To do this properly, she might need to move away from Cornwall, which I can't imagine happening. First and foremost, she must crack on with a business plan and identify the key things that are going make her principal idea a success. She must then really focus on delivering it.

The gaps in Dan and Lucy's skill set are huge. They have no business, commercial, marketing or sales skills whatsoever, and they also have very little drive. In business this makes for a dangerous combination.

## Budgeting

We set Dan and Lucy a budget of £88 per week (£352 per month) for food, clothes and other household goods. If they stick to it, they could save around £600 per month. But Dan has never really budgeted for anything, or concerned himself about keeping within financial constraints. He actually needs to be generating around £1,000 to £1,500 per week, but it might as well be ten times that figure because he's unlikely to achieve either. Talk about money and Dan glazes over. Talk about his work and he really comes alive.

I also fear that when the sun's out and the surf's up, they'll head for the sea rather than take their business ideas forward. I've lived in Cornwall – I know what it's like. Time slips by and it's hard to focus on financial targets. The concept of time management is totally alien to Dan and Lucy.

If they are to hit their target and improve their financial security, this delightful couple will have to change their way of life for two years. I really hope they manage it, but I'm not convinced they can. Their habits are deeply ingrained and I suspect they won't like the impact the change would make on their laid-back lifestyle.

Given their circumstances, Dan and Lucy appear to be long shots in the experiment to pay off their mortgage within two years.

### RENÉ'S SUMMARY

Dan and Lucy opted out of the financial rat race and instead chose to live a pure, organic and ecologically sound life. Yet recently they decided to take on quite a big mortgage, which has drawn them back into the world they left behind. I'm sure that's not where they want to be, and I'm not convinced they're going to thrive in that sort of environment.

## Heather and Chloe Wolsey-Ottaway

Heather and Chloe are in their mid-30s and have recently moved to Cornwall from Scotland. Heather is a social worker and Chloe is a writer and artist. They have a mortgage of £90,000.

Heather and Chloe

Here we have a couple who have reached a turning point in their lives. Heather would like to move out of her pressurized and emotionally demanding job in social work to develop a business as a life coach, while Chloe would dearly love to devote all her time to writing books and developing her artistic talents.

They are very sociable people, have a wide network of friends, and know that they need to clear their mortgage in order to have any chance of living the life they really want. In an ideal world, the couple would like to divide their time between the UK and France.

When they first got together, Heather was over £14,000 in debt, so they decided to live on her salary and use Chloe's income to pay off the debt. They lived within a budget and were able to tighten their belts when necessary. They also made extra money by running a business called Beyond Chaos, which offered a 'life laundry' service, helping people to declutter and reorganize their lives which they ran alongside their day jobs. This made good use of Chloe's DIY skills and her ability to organize and motivate people.

Once they were back on an even keel, they moved to Cornwall, where their financial roles reversed. But Chloe doesn't want to be living off Heather for much longer. Having had some short stories published, she would like to be a fulltime writer and artist. However, the couple have worked out that they need an extra £900 per week to do this – the equivalent of around £47,000 per annum. Given that they have been in debt and worked their way out of it, I feel that they really have the potential to pay off their mortgage early.

## Money-making ideas

Having previous experience of running a business is always an advantage. Beyond Chaos had a successful track record, but they hadn't tried to scale it up, so building it now might be an issue.

Chloe also wants to run a children's entertainment company that will do birthday parties at which she can use her painting and story telling skills. This idea certainly has legs, but is constrained by two things – children's parties invariably happen at weekends (i.e. just two days a week), and most of them are held in the afternoon, so the couple will struggle to do more than two parties per weekend.

Another plan is for Chloe to get some of her stories published and sell more art. This will mean approaching publishers and galleries, so she must do some research. If she can come up with a theme and produce a series of books on it, she may well be able to make more money than she would by producing the odd book here and there.

The final idea is for Heather to train as a life coach and develop this into a business. It is the least developed of their business ideas because Heather will be going into it from a standing start and has few contacts and little or no network in this area.

My impression is that even if Chloe's writing and painting contribute £10,000 per annum and Heather's life coaching £5,000 per annum, the target of £90,000 is still looking a long way off.

## Budgeting

In addition to their various money-making activities, Heather and Chloe will have to budget properly. They have a mixed background in terms of financial discipline, so it will be interesting to see how they respond to serious cutbacks. I feel that it isn't something they have properly considered in the past.

Their income is pretty straightforward, if not a little one-sided. Heather brings in £1,645 per month and Chloe £42, giving a total monthly income of £1,687.

Their regular monthly expenditure, including almost £600 on their mortgage, is £826. By the time they add on food, petrol, clothes, dogs and so forth, they are up to £2,182.

We gave them a weekly budget of £91 (£364 per month) and they are sticking to it. (I did suggest that getting rid of their dogs would save around £100 per month, but they didn't seem to like the idea!)

I like Heather and Chloe a lot. They are great fun, have drive and determination, and are full of enthusiasm. They need serious help on the numbers, as well as in determining the detail of a sales and marketing plan – especially for the decluttering business.

Another concern is that they just do not think in a business-like manner. My fear is that when it comes to executing their plans, they will just be too woolly and undisciplined, and will revert to doing what they feel comfortable with, rather than being driven by the numbers they need to achieve. However, I believe that if they really want to fulfil their ambitions, they will succeed. Of all the contributors to this experiment, Heather and Chloe are applying themselves better than anyone and deserve success.

## RENÉ'S SUMMARY

Heather and Chloe are quite a committed couple. They are industrious, hardworking and can be very focused – in the recent past they have paid off a debt of £14,000. One of my concerns is that they've recently moved from Edinburgh, where they were part of an active community, knew people and were connected, to Cornwall where they don't have the same understanding of the area. That will be a challenge. But I'm convinced that they can work really hard and focus on paying off their mortgage. I just wonder whether they can think big enough.

# Chapter 1
# **Why Pay Off Your Mortgage Early?**

**This book** is about ways in which you can pay off your mortgage early. But why would you want to do that? After all, the burden often gets less as the years go by and you can manage, can't you? Well, that might be so, but wouldn't you like to do more than 'manage'? Wouldn't you like to have that mortgage money so that you could do something new and exciting? This book will show you how.

Most of us got our first mortgage when we were playing Monopoly: having bought property or built hotels in the wrong place, or sacrificed too much in pursuit of all four stations on the board, we got into financial difficulties and had to borrow from the 'bank'.

In the real world a mortgage involves large monthly payments being taken from our bank accounts, a depressing annual statement that shows we have made little or no headway in paying off the basic loan, and a feeling that, one of these days, we really must get round to changing to a better rate.

Unlike people in continental Europe, who tend to rent property rather than buy, we Brits have a long-standing love affair with home ownership. It is often said that an Englishman's home is his castle, but the Scots, Welsh and Irish are just as keen to have the deeds to their own pile of bricks and mortar. The principles within this book apply to Scotland and Northern Ireland as well as England and Wales, but there can be differences in the way properties are bought and sold in Scotland. Very different rules can apply in the Irish Republic, too. In recent years property and DIY have become national obsessions, as evidenced by all the television programmes devoted to development and makeovers.

This is perhaps understandable given the meteoric rise in residential property values, the average property price having almost doubled in five years.

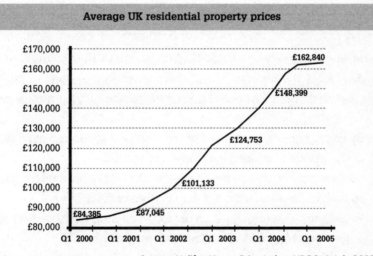

Average UK residential property prices

Source: Halifax House Price Index, HBOS, 1 July 2005

For most of us, house purchase is only possible with the assistance of a mortgage loan, and unburdening ourselves of that loan is an aspiration that few have the luxury of achieving more quickly than the usual 25-year term.

An October 2004 survey by HSBC found that 70% of home owners would be impressed if their friends revealed they had paid off their mortgage early. Two-thirds would be eager to know how they had managed it, 50% said they would be jealous, and a mere 6% would conclude it was a waste of money.

## Avoid that interest

René says

Work out exactly **how much interest** you will pay over the current term of the mortgage. The majority of this huge amount can be avoided just by paying off **your mortgage early.** Keep reminding yourself of this **'interest-free'** bonus!

## Reasons to pay off early

Your home is likely to be the largest purchase that you will ever make, and it is natural to want to own it outright as soon as possible. But there are other good reasons for paying off your mortgage:

- By paying up before the end of the loan period you can save tens of thousands of pounds in interest payments.
- The average mortgage term is longer than most jail sentences, so imagine how liberating it is to be free of debt.
- Paying off the mortgage is an obvious first step for those seeking to retire early and set off on new adventures.
- Being free of mortgage repayments means having more money to spend on the better things in life, or to put into higher yielding investments.
- Getting rid of one home loan could make room for another – perhaps on a cottage in Provence or a villa in Spain. (Among our contributors, the Holleymans had already bought investment property overseas, and everyone else, except Dan and Lucy, was keen to do so.)

'What can be added to the happiness
of a man who is in health, out of debt,
and has a clear conscience?'
Adam Smith, US poet and novelist (1872–1906)

In recent years we have seen an explosion of personal debt in the UK. It's become the norm for students to have debts of tens of thousands of pounds, and for people to get bigger and bigger mortgages as house prices have increased. My worry is that huge numbers of people have got used to living with debt and have given little serious thought to how they will repay it. House prices may not rise indefinitely, and that puts an awful lot of people at risk if they have overborrowed on their home or run up hefty debts on personal loans and credit cards.

The tipping point may come when the UK economy falters and jobs become at risk. Then people will stop spending and borrowing, and start to think about repaying debt rather than adding to it. The problem may be that within that doomsday scenario the extent of individual debt may have gone too far for some to rectify without incurring huge losses.

Of course, it may not turn out like this, but I'm a firm believer in being safe rather than sorry. I recommend that you start paying off that debt sooner rather than later, and start considering ways to pay off your mortgage early.

# Chapter 2
# Know Your Mortgage

**Put simply**, a mortgage is a secured loan provided specifically to finance the purchase of property. In most instances this means that the lender will register a charge against your home as security for a loan provided to assist with its purchase. If you fail to keep up repayments on a mortgage, the lender can repossess your house and sell it to recoup the loan.

## DID YOU KNOW?

**The word 'mortgage' is a French legal term that translates literally as 'dead pledge'. This means that it is an absolute right to something (the property), but does not come into effect provided certain conditions are met (repayments are made and the debt subsequently exhausted).**

## Types of mortgage

There are two main types of mortgage. The first consists of capital repayments as well as the interest due on the loan; the other consists solely of interest repayments, leaving the capital to be repaid separately at the end of the term.

## Capital and interest mortgage

Also known as a repayment mortgage, this is the most popular type of home loan. The capital is gradually paid back to the lender each month along with any interest due. In the early years the repayments consist mainly of interest, but the capital element increases as the loan progresses until, towards the end of the loan, the capital repayments outweigh the interest, as illustrated below.

As long as payments are maintained, the mortgage is guaranteed to be paid off at maturity, and, in the unlikely event that interest rates do not alter, the monthly repayments will stay the same.

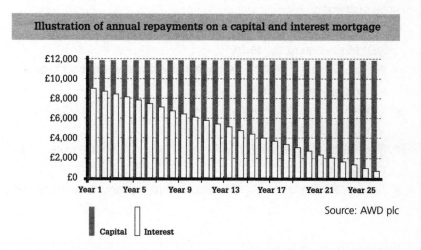

Illustration of annual repayments on a capital and interest mortgage

Source: AWD plc

Capital ☐ Interest

The following is a schedule of repayments based upon a capital and interest mortgage of £150,000 borrowed at a fixed rate of 6% over 25 years.

The repayments are £11,374 per annum, which equates to just under £950 per month.

The initial annual interest repayment can be calculated as £150,000 x 6.0% = £9,000. The additional £2,374 represents the capital repaid in the first year.

At the beginning of year two, the balance outstanding is reduced to £147,266 and the annual interest repayment is reduced to £8,836 (£147,266 x 6.0% = £8,836). The remaining £2,898 is put towards the repayment of the capital (£11,374 total repayment less £8,836 interest paid). This is repeated until year 25, when the loan is repaid in full.

If death occurs before the mortgage is repaid, the outstanding balance will become a debt against the deceased's estate. Most lenders will make it a condition of the loan that an appropriate amount of life assurance cover is obtained to provide for the mortgage to be paid off in the event of death.

*Pros and cons*

✔ Capital and interest mortgages are guaranteed to pay off the loan at the end of the term.

✔ The lender may agree to changes in the term of the mortgage or allow 'payment holidays'.

✔ You will generally pay less in total interest charges in comparison to an interest-only mortgage.

✗ There is no prospect of an additional lump sum being available at the end of the term.

✗ The monthly repayments are weighted in favour of interest in the early years.

## Interest-only mortgage

As the name suggests, with an interest-only mortgage, the borrower's repayments consist solely of the interest due on the amount advanced, and provision must be made separately to repay the capital at the end of the term. This type of mortgage is commonly known by the name of the investment vehicle used to fund the repayment, so may be called an endowment-, pension- or ISA- (Individual Savings Account) linked mortgage. As the repayments to the lender do not include any repayment of capital, the amount of the debt remains constant and is the same in year 25 as it is in year one.

Repayments on this type of mortgage are represented in the chart below, which assumes that the interest rate applicable to the loan remains constant throughout (which is unlikely).

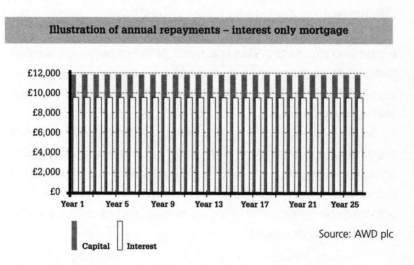

**Illustration of annual repayments – interest only mortgage**

Source: AWD plc

The monthly interest repayments can be calculated simply by using the following formula:

$$\frac{\text{Amount borrowed x interest rate}}{12 \text{ months}}$$

If we assume an interest-only mortgage of £150,000 borrowed at a fixed rate of 6.0%, the monthly repayments can be calculated as follows:

$$\frac{£150,000 \times 6\%}{12} = \frac{£9,000}{12} = £750 \text{ per month}$$

Remember that this formula is used only to calculate the interest due on the loan and does not include any contribution towards repaying the capital sum borrowed. In this instance a separate monthly saving of about £333 per month is required into an investment plan, such as an ISA, in order to pay off the £150,000 capital.

Interest-only mortgages were really popular in the 1970s and 1980s, a boom time for home purchase fuelled partly by the Conservative government's 'right to buy' initiative on council houses. The popularity of interest-only loans can be attributed to the fact that they often appeared cheaper in comparison to capital and interest repayment mortgages. This is a result of the growth rate assumptions made on associated stockmarket-linked endowment plans, many of which have failed to materialize, prompting claims of mis-selling in recent years.

As with capital and interest mortgages, if death occurs before the mortgage is repaid, the outstanding balance will become a debt against the deceased's estate. Some repayment vehicles, such as endowments, include an element of life cover, but where this is not present, most lenders will make it a condition of the loan that additional life cover is bought.

*Pros and cons*

✔ If the investment performance of the repayment vehicle is favourable, it may be possible to reduce the term of the loan, or there may be an excess lump sum available at maturity.

✔ Repayments tend to be cheaper in comparison to capital and interest mortgages, although this is dependent on the assumed growth rate of the associated repayment vehicle and may prove to be a false economy if the endowment, ISA or pension does not increase at the expected rate.

✗ There is no guarantee that the chosen repayment vehicle will be sufficient to repay the loan.

✗ ISAs and personal pensions can only be taken out on a single life (although for joint mortgages the loan may be supported by two separate policies).

✗ You will generally pay more in total interest charges with an interest-only loan.

## A word of caution

It may seem blindingly obvious, but it needs to be said: it is a very bad idea to overstretch yourself with the size of mortgage you take out. As advertisements often remind us (at breathtaking speed): 'Your home may be at risk if you do not keep up repayments on your mortgage or any other loan secured upon it.'

While this may seem like common sense, it is worth remembering that interest rates were as high as 15.4% only a decade or so ago, and that negative equity (see page 52-53) became commonplace when the value of properties fell below the price paid for them. Interestingly, that situation was preceded by a period of rapid growth during the late 1980s – not dissimilar to what is going on at the present time.

According to the Council of Mortgage Lenders, the amount that is being borrowed in relation to the income of the borrower shows a worrying trend, as illustrated below:

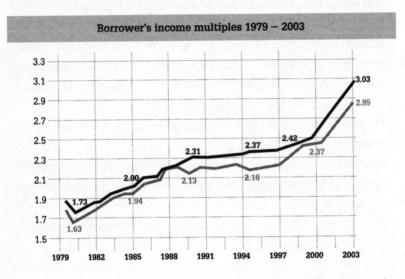

Source: Council of Mortgage Lenders

Lenders justify the increased level of borrowing by pointing out that interest rates are at a relatively low point in comparison to the long-term average, so there is no significant increase in affordability. However, in the UK there is an unprecedented amount of unsecured personal debt (largely through credit card borrowing) and, as shown on page 76, a 1% rise in interest rates can make a considerable difference. We should not forget that repossessions were common following the last residential property boom.

Mortgages are long-term commitments, and while they may be affordable now, what would happen if your income falls? You may think that this is unlikely, but take a moment to consider how you would cope if you lost your job and had to take a drop in income, or, worse still, if you became ill and couldn't work, or had to cease work to look after a dependant. Would your mortgage still be affordable?

# How to protect your mortgage

Like any other asset, it is important to ensure that your property and your mortgage are protected against all eventualities. This section looks at some of the plans that are available to help cope with a range of possible events that all have an impact upon your ability to meet mortgage repayments.

## Life cover

Lenders always recommend – and in many cases insist – that borrowers arrange an appropriate policy so that the mortgage will be repaid in the event of the borrower's death, rather than it being a burden to their dependants or estate. In the case of a joint mortgage, it is particularly important that life cover is obtained for the main breadwinner, to avoid forcing dependants into selling the home simply to repay the bank or building society.

There are many types of life cover available, and the most suitable depends upon the type of mortgage you have. Some endowment mortgages will include life assurance cover, whereas ISA- and pension-linked mortgages usually do not. Remember, if you have an interest-only mortgage, the amount you owe the lender is likely to remain constant, whereas with a capital and interest repayment mortgage your debt will diminish throughout the term. Level term cover – where the amount of life cover remains constant throughout the period of cover – is usually sufficient for interest-only mortgages, while a policy known as a mortgage protection plan is generally the most cost-efficient for those where the balance is decreasing.

If you are in good health and have a life assurance policy that has been in existence for many years, it is worth shopping around to see if cover can be arranged more cheaply as the cost varies considerably between providers, a fact that is not lost on lenders, whose rates are often among the most expensive. The rate also fluctuates according to general life expectancy. In the 1980s, when

Aids was feared to be far more widespread than has been the case, the cost of life assurance cover was generally higher than now. You can find out if your current plan is competitive by checking with an online broker or an independent financial adviser (see page 56).

Life cover is almost always underwritten – which means that an individual's personal health, age and circumstances are all taken into account to determine the premium. This requires your state of health to be assessed on application, and the plan will be more expensive if you have suffered ill health.

Where mortgages are taken out in joint names, life cover is often arranged on a joint basis and will pay out on the death of either policy holder.

### CASE STUDY

Paddy MacVean is a self-employed builder, so his job security relies more than most on remaining fit and healthy enough to work. At the beginning of the TV series he had no pension to speak of, and very little life cover. By paying off his mortgage early he will be able to make better provision for his retirement and ensure that his family won't suffer financially if his income falls.

### INSURANCE OR ASSURANCE?

What's the difference between life insurance and life assurance? It depends on the term of the plan. Insurance refers to cover for an event that *might* happen, such as a car accident, while assurance is the provision of cover for an event that is *certain* to happen, such as death. A policy that will run for a fixed period of years is a life insurance plan, whereas a 'whole of life' contract, which pays out on death whenever it occurs, is life assurance.

## Accident, sickness and unemployment cover

Also known by its initials, ASU insurance provides the borrower with a degree of protection against mortgage repayments becoming unaffordable in the event of redundancy or not being able to work due to an accident or long-term sickness. These policies provide replacement income, usually for a period of up to two years or until the claimant returns to work, if earlier. There may also be a delay before payments begin, known as a 'deferred period', which helps to keep the cost down and usually lasts for 3, 6 or 12 months.

ASU is probably the most controversial mortgage-linked protection policy because its benefits tend to be paid for only a short, fixed period of time and the cost is considered by many to be poor value for money. Added to that, most people made redundant do everything in their power to rectify the situation as soon as possible, so the benefit is rarely paid for a long time.

It is important to check the definition of 'redundancy', especially if you work in an industry where contract working is commonplace.

## Buildings insurance

Like life cover, buildings insurance will be a condition of your mortgage. After all, the lender would not want to lend a lot of money on an uninsured property only to have it fall down and leave them with a large loan secured against a pile of rubble. Of course, you probably wouldn't be overjoyed at the prospect either.

Buildings insurance provides protection against a range of events, including fire, earthquake, storms, accidental damage and subsidence, and is available from most major insurance companies and brokers. Again, your lender may have arranged cover for you, in which case it is worth checking how competitive the cost of your policy is, because the lender will have received a commission for arranging the plan.

## Contents insurance

While contents insurance is not strictly required to protect a mortgage, it gives peace of mind – and it is never a good idea to economize by not adequately insuring the contents of your property.

Contents insurance usually covers events such as fire, theft or damage to items while in the home, and is often obtained from the same provider as the buildings insurance. In fact, many companies offer a discount when both types of insurance are taken out at the same time. Take care to specify high-value items, such as engagement rings or works of art, separately within the policy.

## Critical illness cover

First introduced in the 1980s, critical illness cover pays out a lump sum benefit if you are diagnosed as suffering from a specified serious illness. It is a sad fact that almost all of us can think of somebody who has been diagnosed with cancer, or who has suffered a stroke or a heart attack. Thankfully, advances in medical treatment and technology mean that many are eventually able to recover from these diseases.

Consider for a moment the effect that a critical illness would have on you and your family: the last thing you'd want to worry about is paying the mortgage. A critical illness protection policy will provide a valuable benefit just when it is most required to help you through a recovery period, to fund medical treatment, or simply to take the recuperation break that the doctor orders. In many respects critical illness cover is more important than life cover, and it is another area where economies should be avoided.

## SERIOUS ILLNESS STATISTICS

- One in three men and one in five women currently aged 30 will have a stroke, cancer or heart attack before the age of 65.
- One in three people in Britain will be diagnosed with cancer at some point in their life.
- In the UK a heart attack strikes every two minutes.
- One in nine women will develop breast cancer at some point in their lives.

Sources: ERC Frankona Reinsurance; Imperial Cancer Research Fund; Chest Heart Stroke Association (1998); Office for National Statistics

Critical illness cover can be arranged as a stand-alone policy, although it is often offered as an additional option attached to a life cover plan. It is not uncommon for the two elements to be combined so that one policy will pay out on the death of either one of two joint policy holders, or in the event of a critical illness being diagnosed in either of them.

### Income protection

Also known as permanent health insurance, income protection provides much greater cover than accident, sickness and unemployment plans, with benefits often paid until retirement.

Income protection plans are designed to provide a regular benefit to replace income in the event that the policy holder is unable to work through ill health. Benefits are restricted to a percentage of salary previously earned so as not to be a disincentive to returning to work. The maximum is usually around 60% of previous salary.

As with ASU cover (see page 49), there is a deferred period following a claim, after which benefit payments begin. These are usually set at a level that matches the long-term sickness arrangements of the employer, and can last anywhere from four weeks to two years. The length of the deferred period chosen can have a dramatic effect on the cost of the plan.The advantage of income protection over ASU cover is that the benefit is potentially payable for a much longer period of time and can be considered as true income replacement. ASU is little more than a stopgap. Income protection contracts are often offered by employers as part of an executive remuneration package, as they can also insure against the cost of providing long-term incapacity benefits to employees.

An income protection policy is highly complementary to a critical illness plan, and together they provide comprehensive protection against the effects of serious debilitating conditions.

Almost all the contributors to the TV series were underinsured in some shape or form. A little extra cost now can save a lot of heartache and sleepless nights later on because so many of our plans are based on our income. Just think about what you would lose if you had no income for 12 months or more. Your house? Your car? Holidays? Your partner?! The list might be endless ...

Adequate insurance cover is crucial. As an adviser, I have seen the price people pay when they are underinsured – at a financial level, it is madness; at a human level, it is sadness. Of our contributors, Dan and Lucy might have to sell their house if catastrophe strikes; Duncan would go into a tailspin; and Sean and Anne-Marie would need root and branch pruning of their home and lifestyle.

## Negative equity

'Equity' is the term given to the difference between the value of your home and the amount of your mortgage. If your property is worth less than the amount that you owe your lender, you are said to be in 'negative equity'. This is a problem because if you attempt to move house, you may find that you owe your lender thousands of pounds more than your property is worth.

You might think that negative equity is a problem from the past, particularly the period between 1989 and 1994, but articles in the *Guardian*, the *Financial Times* and the *Scotsman* have recently been warning that it may be about to make a comeback. It is commonplace nowadays to see headlines announcing 'House Price Weakness' or 'Mortgage Completions Falling'. The following example shows how negative equity can happen.

**An example of negative equity**

| August 2004 | August 2006 |
|---|---|
| Purchase price **£150,00** | Value **£127,500** (-15%) |
| Mortgage **£142,500** | Mortgage **£142,500** |
| Equity **£7,500** | Negative equity **-£15,000** |

Source: AWD plc

In the four years from 1989 to 1993 property prices fell by 13% nationally, and around 27% in London and the south-east (following a booming housing market that saw prices increase by an average of 34% in 1988). As a result, about 1.8 million home owners who had bought during the boom were left in a negative equity position. Currently, there are fears that low interest rates and the increase in popularity of buy-to-let investments has forced prices well above their historical average to an artificial high.

In 1991 some 75,540 homes were repossessed after owners defaulted on mortgage payments. To make matters even worse, after each home was sold by the building society, the previous owners were presented with a bill for any shortfall in the value realized compared to the amount borrowed. When you also consider that in 2005 unsecured personal debt is at record levels, it is easy to understand why there is concern.

If you find yourself in a negative equity situation and you are desperate to move house, your circumstances have changed or you have a significant amount of other debt secured against your property, it is imperative to speak to your lender as soon as possible. Banks and building societies much prefer working with a borrower to reach an amicable long-term solution rather than repossessing the property. They may even allow you to move house and transfer the debt to another property, especially if you are moving to something cheaper. Prompt action can turn negative equity from a serious problem into a manageable annoyance.

## Knowledge is power

An alarming point came out during the making of the TV series that this book accompanies: very few of the contributors had given any serious consideration to paying off the capital element of their mortgage. Almost as bad, most contributors didn't know what type of mortgage they had, and they certainly weren't aware of the risks of an interest-only mortgage and the possibility that they might not own their house at the end of the loan period. Scary.

Make sure you're not in the same position. Find out what sort of mortgage you have, how much you pay each month and where you'll stand at the end of the loan period. Knowledge is power, and power gives you the freedom to choose a life free of debt and do what gives you pleasure.

> *'There is only one good, knowledge,
> and one evil, ignorance.'*
> Socrates (469 BC-399 BC)

# Chapter 3
# Repaying the Capital on an Interest-Only Mortgage

**In the 1980s and 1990s** the vast majority of interest-only mortgages were supported by low-cost endowment policies, in many cases with the proceeds of the policy assigned to the lender. It was rare to find mortgages linked to other plans such as personal pensions, unit trusts or PEPs (Personal Equity Plans, the predecessors of ISAs). In fact, many lenders at the time would not entertain the notion of underpinning a loan with anything other than an endowment.

These days, lenders are much more flexible in their approach, and in many instances do not insist upon seeing proof of any repayment vehicle at all. It is important not to underestimate the significance of your chosen investment vehicle in paying off your mortgage, and to remain vigilant towards its performance. Regular reviews should be undertaken at least every year or so, and preferably with an independent financial adviser.

## QUESTIONS TO ASK YOUR MORTGAGE BROKER

**1. Are you independent and is your advice based upon the 'whole market'?**

Some brokers offer advice on the products from just one lender and some are tied to a restricted panel of lenders. Truly independent advisers will consider what is offered by all lenders – the whole of the market – before deciding on what is most appropriate for you.

### 2. Are you (and your firm) regulated by the Financial Services Authority?

If you receive advice from an authorized person or firm you will also have access to complaints procedures and compensation schemes if things don't go as expected. A quick check of whether or not an individual or firm is authorized can be made on the FSA website (see page 186).

### 3. What qualifications do you have?

Since 2004, the FSA requires anyone who gives advice on mortgages to be professionally qualified. There are two qualifications accredited as 'appropriate' by the Financial Services Skills Council: the Certificate in Mortgage Advice and Practice (CeMap) from the Institute of Financial Services, and the Mortgage Qualification (CF6) from the Chartered Insurance Institute.

### 4. Can you explain (in writing) how you are paid?

Some mortgage brokers will charge you a fee either payable directly or added to the mortgage. Check that you are happy with the amount of this fee and that it is commensurate with the work involved – a fee of around £100 to £200 per hour is not unusual. Most mortgage brokers will also receive a so-called procuration fee from the lender for placing your mortgage with them. In addition, if you are taking out extra contracts linked to the mortgage – such as buildings and contents insurance, life assurance, or an accident, sickness and unemployment policy – it is likely that some or all of these will pay commission to your broker. It is important to understand how much your broker is being paid and by whom – if it sounds like too much, say so. If total fees for a relatively straightforward mortgage of £100,000 go into thousands of pounds, that clearly feels too expensive.

### 5. Will you provide me with information or advice?

It is important to understand whether you are simply being told about the mortgages that are available or whether you are receiving advice about which may be most suitable for you. If you do not seek advice and something goes wrong, you will have less redress than if your personal needs have been assessed.

'A financial adviser is someone who invests your money for you until it's all gone.'
Woody Allen, US film director (1935–)

# Endowment policies

An endowment policy is a savings plan that also provides life assurance cover. When used in conjunction with a mortgage, it is designed to pay off the loan at maturity, or on the death of the policy holder if this occurs before that date. According to the Association of British Insurers, at the time of writing (2005) there are about 9.5 million endowment policies linked to mortgages in the United Kingdom.

The term 'endowment' encompasses many different types of plan that contain some fundamental differences, and it is important to identify what type of policy you have. It is advisable to seek independent advice on endowments, especially when dealing with older policies, as the terminology can be confusing. Indeed, when asked, call-centre staff at many insurance companies may not fully appreciate the distinctions and nuances in the different types of contract.

## Full endowments

A full endowment policy contains guarantees that the sum assured will be paid out in full on maturity or in the event of death. It is sometimes referred to as a non-profit or without profit endowment, and such policies are generally considered to be expensive and poor value because of the sheer cost involved – if indeed you can actually find them. These days, insurance companies are choosing not to offer guarantees because they are looking to reduce their liabilities in the future.

## With-profit endowments

A with-profit policy consist of three elements:

• A sum assured that the insurer will pay at maturity.
• Annual (or reversionary) bonuses that are added to the policy value

each year. (A reversionary bonus is one that, once added, cannot be taken away.)

- A terminal bonus that is added at maturity.

The overall aim of with-profit policies is to smooth out the fluctuations in returns associated with stock market investments.

During the year, the insurance company will pool the contributions made by all policy holders and invest them in a mixture of assets, including company shares and property. At the end of each year, the company calculates the surplus of assets over liabilities (the total of the sums assured) and decides how much money it wishes to retain in the fund to strengthen it against poor performance in future years, and how much money to allocate to policy holders as annual bonuses. Once added, these bonuses cannot be taken away.

The terminal bonus is a discretionary payment that can represent a significant proportion of the total proceeds of the plan. It is calculated when the benefits are paid out (either at maturity or on the death of the policy holder) and is designed to ensure that the eventual pay-out is broadly in line with the returns of the underlying fund throughout the term of the policy.

As with full endowment policies, the proceeds are guaranteed to match the amount of the loan, and in practice should be considerably higher. This is the most expensive form of endowment and, as a result, is not popular with borrowers.

## Low-cost endowments

This type of endowment policy represents the majority of those held by borrowers. These endowments have a lower sum assured than the mortgage amount, but include an additional element of decreasing term assurance cover so that in the event of the policy holder's death, the proceeds will match the outstanding loan.

Where plans are held to maturity, it is expected that the future growth of the underlying investments will result in additional annual and terminal bonuses, which, when added to the sum assured, will (it is hoped) make up the amount of the loan at maturity – but there is no guarantee of this.

The amount of the monthly contribution is based upon the growth rate assumed at the outset. If a reasonably conservative growth rate has been used, there should be sufficient funds at maturity to repay the loan and, with luck, provide a surplus. This is detailed below for a mortgage of £150,000.

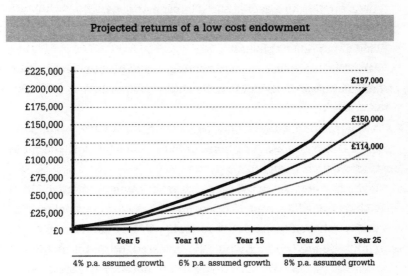

Projected returns of a low cost endowment

Source: AWD plc

Most low-cost endowment policies were taken out while interest rates were much higher than they are today, and the stock market was regularly producing double-digit returns. Just as mortgage interest rates have fallen, so have the prospects for investment returns. As a result, the UK insurance industry has agreed with the Financial Services Authority (FSA) to ensure that lower growth rates are used in endowment benefit illustrations and that investors are warned of any potential shortfall.

Insurance companies have been sending out letters advising policy holders of the possible future performance of their endowment policies and, where appropriate, encouraging them to make additional arrangements to cover any projected shortfall.

There are three main options open to endowment owners. They can:

- Make changes to the mortgage loan, such as switching the amount of the projected shortfall by converting from an interest-only mortgage, to a capital and interest mortgage.
- Start an additional savings plan so that the money saved can be used to pay off any shortfall.
- Vary the endowment policy, extending the term of the endowment (and mortgage) or topping up the endowment plan.

Not surprisingly, these endowment problems have prompted a great deal of bad press, and borrowers have increasingly sought to restructure their mortgages.

If you find yourself in the predicament of having a shortfall, there may be grounds for a complaint against the person or company who originally sold you the endowment policy if they did not explain to you how the endowment would be invested, or that it would not necessarily pay off your mortgage in full because it depended on investment performance. For more information contact the FSA, the independent watchdog set up by the government to regulate financial services in the UK and protect the rights of retail customers. Its website (see page 186) contains useful information to assist you in deciding whether you have a valid complaint and how to proceed with it.

It is pointless burying your head in the sand and hoping that any shortfall in the value of your endowment will just go away – it's a big issue. One good thing about mortgages is that they run for a long time. This can work to your advantage in that the sooner you take action to get your mortgage repaid, the better. If you don't, you may be left to pick up the tab for thousands of pounds of shortfall that you never expected.

*Pros and cons*

✔ At maturity, your endowment may be worth more than the outstanding loan and may give you a tax-free surplus.

✘ The charges tend to be high in the early years, and your endowment may be poor value if surrendered before the end of the term.

✘ Your endowment may not perform as well as originally anticipated and when it matures there may be a shortfall which you will need to make up yourself.

## What type of endowment do you have?

Identifying what type of endowment you have is not straightforward. Full endowments are very rare, and the majority of these were taken out in the 1970s and early 1980s. Many have already matured or will be very close to maturity.

More bewildering is the distinction between with-profit endowments and low-cost endowments. With-profit endowments are rare compared to low-cost endowments, yet many low-cost endowments are invested in with-profit funds, and are often mistakenly referred to as with-profit endowments. Confused? It's easy to see why.

Your policy document should help you to assess what you have. As a rough guide, if your policy was taken out after 1988 it is likely to be a low-cost endowment. Another sign that you have a low-cost policy is that you should have received correspondence from the policy provider advising whether or not your endowment is on course to match the mortgage debt. If in doubt, gather as much documentation and correspondence as you can lay your hands on and seek independent advice.

*'There are worse things in life than death: have you ever spent the evening with an insurance salesman?'*
Woody Allen, US film director (1935–)

## Switch for the better?

Since insurance companies have been writing to policy holders and advising them of potential shortfalls, many borrowers have sought to restructure their mortgages. One popular strategy has been to switch all or part of the mortgage from an interest-only basis to a capital and interest repayment basis, which is guaranteed to be paid off at the end of the term. In this case, and if it is affordable, it is best to keep the endowment contract as a savings plan. Indeed, wherever possible, it is generally advisable to hold endowment policies until maturity.

## Cashing in

Some people opt to cash in their endowment policy and use the accumulated proceeds to pay off part of their mortgage, but this is not always the best option. If you were to cash in within the first five years, you might not even get back the amount that you had paid out in contributions. Endowment contracts can be poor value in the early years when the majority of the charges are taken from the plan, before gradually becoming better value and, with luck, providing an excess lump sum at the end of the term.

If you do decide to encash an endowment, take care to bear the following points in mind:

- Endowment proceeds are protected from tax by a relief known as 'qualifying status', which may be put in jeopardy if surrendered.

- As well as being a savings vehicle, the endowment policy is also likely to be providing the required life assurance to ensure that the mortgage is repaid in the event of early death. This cover may be a condition of the loan and will need to be replaced. Where a borrower's health has deteriorated since the endowment was taken out, replacement life cover may be more expensive.
- When held for the full term, endowment maturity proceeds offer such good value in comparison to the amount realized on surrender that there are now investors willing to buy them from borrowers who would otherwise encash. If your policy is more than six or seven years old and is invested in a with-profit fund, it is advisable to check if it is saleable. The Association of Policy Market Makers (see page 186) can provide details of companies who will purchase an endowment from you. If an endowment is sold rather than surrendered, the policy proceeds will be paid out to whoever has purchased the policy either at maturity or in the event of the original policy holder's death, if earlier.

Only one or two of our contributors had endowment policies. On the basis that something is better than nothing, this was interesting. It illustrated that not many of them had given serious consideration as to how they might pay back the capital element of their mortgage. In the main, endowments have had their day, but this begs the question: if endowments aren't being used to pay off mortgages, what are?

## Personal pensions

Mortgages linked to pensions became popular following the intro-
duction of individual personal pensions in 1988. Personal pensions
are private arrangements designed to provide lump sum and
income benefits at retirement. Contributions attract income tax
relief at the policy holder's highest tax rate and build up in a
favourable tax environment. Under current legislation, benefits can
be taken from age 50, and up to 25% of the fund may be paid as a
tax-free lump sum, which for pension-linked mortgages is used to
repay an interest-only loan. The remaining 75% of the fund at
retirement must be used to provide income benefits. A life cover
policy, which may be linked to the pension, is also required to
ensure that the mortgage is repaid in the event of early death.

Contributions of up to £3,600 per annum gross (£2,808 net of
basic rate tax relief at 22%) may be made without reference to
earnings. This limit applies to total pension contributions, so if you
have various pension arrangements, take care that total contributions to all schemes are calculated.

Contributions in excess of £3,600 are currently restricted to a
percentage of earnings in any tax year according to age, subject to
a maximum wage (£105,600 in the current tax year 2005/6). The
percentage contributions are detailed below.

| Maximum permitted pension contributions 2005/6 | |
|---|---|
| Age at 6 April | Maximum contributions as a percentage of earnings |
| 35 or less | 17.5% |
| 36–45 | 20% |
| 46–50 | 25% |
| 51–55 | 30% |
| 56–60 | 35% |
| 61–74 | 40% |

Source: AWD plc

Contributions are permitted to grow in a tax-privileged environment, free from both income and capital gains tax. Most pensions provide a broad range of investment options covering the main asset classes – such as cash, property, shares and fixed interest investments – as well as managed funds and stock market index trackers.

Some providers also offer external fund links to funds managed by unit trust groups and investment houses. With a range of fund options available, it is possible to create a bespoke portfolio to match individual requirements in terms of objectives, timescale and attitude to risk.

In the late 1980s pension contributions by basic rate tax payers attracted 25% income tax relief (as opposed to 22% today), and a popular sales technique was to demonstrate how the government could pay for your home. Here's how it worked:

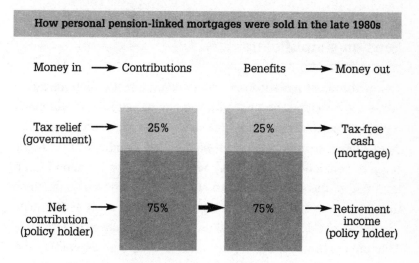

**How personal pension-linked mortgages were sold in the late 1980s**

Money in ⟶ Contributions        Benefits ⟶ Money out

Tax relief ⟶ 25%        25% ⟶ Tax-free cash
(government)                   (mortgage)

Net ⟶ 75%        75% ⟶ Retirement income
contribution                   (policy holder)
(policy holder)

Note: This illustration assumes a historical basic rate of tax of 25% applicable in the late 1980s. At the time of writing (2005), the basic rate of tax, and therefore tax relief, is 22%

Source: AWD plc

As you can see, the real benefit here is the tax relief on your contributions (the money in). The problem is that, in order to pay off a mortgage, you can generally only get 25% of the value of the accumulated fund back out in tax-free cash.

Pension mortgages are generally not the most cost-effective way of funding a mortgage, as only a quarter of each contribution made can be used to provide lump sum benefits, the majority being invested to provide a taxable retirement income. However, as fringe benefits go, a large pension fund isn't to be sneezed at.

## TOP TIP

Start a pension early. Little and often is better than nothing at all.

## Pension simplification

The government has recently embarked on a major reorganization of the UK pension structure with the aim of simplifying the many regimes it currently contains. These changes come into effect on 6 April 2006, known as 'A Day' (Appointed Day), and will affect many areas of pension planning. They will include new simplified funding rules so that individuals can effectively contribute as much as they earn up to an annual limit, which in 2006/07 is set at £215,000.

Overall pension benefits will be capped, initially at £1.5 million. This means that the maximum tax-free cash sum available, and therefore the highest possible mortgage that can be supported by a personal pension, is £375,000.

*Pros and cons*

✔ Contributions attract tax relief at the borrower's highest rate.

✔ The pension fund will grow in a tax-favoured environment.

✔ The cash lump sum will be free of tax.

✔ As well as funding to repay the mortgage, a healthy retirement benefit fund will be accumulated.

✘ Additional life cover is required to ensure that the mortgage is repaid in the event of early death.

✘ The target pension fund must be four times the size of the mortgage, as only 25% of the fund is available as a tax-free cash lump sum. It may therefore prove to be a comparatively expensive way to repay the mortgage.

✘ If the whole of the tax-free cash lump sum is used to redeem the mortgage, it cannot be spent on other things, such as a world cruise.

✘ Pension benefits are only available beyond age 50 (increasing to age 55 under the new simplification proposals), so a pension may not be a suitable repayment for, say, a 25-year-old first-time buyer, as it will require a mortgage term of 30 years or more for the buyer to be able to realize his or her pension.

✘ The highest borrowing that can be supported by a pension will be £375,000 after 6 April 2006 (although this figure will increase as the overall lifetime allowance cap is reviewed).

Again, our experiment threw up the issue that very few of the contributors to the series had any serious pension provision. In the context of mortgages and lifetime financial planning, it could become a major problem for them in the future.

## PEPs and ISAs

Personal Equity Plans (PEPs) and Individual Savings Accounts (ISAs) are tax-favoured savings plans that can be used to support interest-only mortgages.

PEPs were available between 1987 and 1999, and became very popular with borrowers. In April 1999 PEPs were replaced by ISAs, but many PEPs still exist in the hands of investors and retain their tax-favoured status.

An ISA is a tax-efficient investment account that allows eligible individuals to invest specified amounts in each tax year in order to accumulate a fund to match their mortgage liability. The amounts are reviewed periodically by the Chancellor of the Exchequer, and the present allowances are expected to remain until 5 April 2010. ISAs were introduced to encourage long-term savings and simplify the old rules that applied to PEPs and TESSAs (Tax Exempt Special Savings Accounts). When linked to a mortgage, separate life cover is required to ensure that the loan is repaid in the event of early death.

Contributions to ISAs can be made regularly or as a series of one-off payments. There is no fixed investment term, and most providers will allow switches between funds that can be specifically targeted to repay a mortgage. As ISAs are individual accounts, they can be held only in single names, which allows a couple to invest up to £7,000 each a year.

Each tax year you can invest in either one maxi ISA or up to two mini ISAs, which may be divided between stocks and shares and/or cash. The ISA allowance maximum limits for 2005/6 are as follows:

**Maxi ISA**

| | | |
|---|---|---|
| £7,000 in stocks and shares | **or** | £4,000 in stocks and shares and £3,000 (max) in cash |

**Mini ISA**

| | | |
|---|---|---|
| £4,000 in stocks and shares | **and/or** | £3,000 in cash |

As each mini ISA offers investment in one component only, it is possible to have two separate mini ISAs with two different providers. Once you take out a mini ISA, you are restricted, for that tax year, to mini ISA investments.

In practice, if you invest in a cash mini ISA, you are effectively restricting the amount you can invest in stocks and shares from £7,000 to £4,000. If you prefer to spread your investments and have a mixture of stocks and shares and cash, investing in a maxi ISA that combines the two components may offer greater flexibility than two mini ISAs.

The stocks and shares component includes:
- Ordinary shares (equities), UK open-ended investment companies (OEICs) unit trusts and investment trusts.

The cash component includes:
- Instant access deposit accounts from a bank or building society, and National Savings products earning tax-free interest.

Until 2005 it was possible to invest in a third component – life assurance. If you are paying into an ISA with a life assurance component that you held prior to 2005, it may be possible to continue paying into a life assurance component. If in doubt, seek independent advice prior to making any investment decision. ISAs are important because of the 'use it or lose it' rule. If you don't use your ISA allowance in any given year, you lose it for ever.

As with endowments and pensions, the value of the plan will rise and fall in line with the underlying assets. PEPs and ISAs tend to be invested in quite specific investments, such as the shares of UK or European companies. Concentrated investments like these tend to be higher risk than more diversified managed or mixed funds, but offer a higher potential return.

As there is no fixed term, the speed at which the mortgage can be repaid depends on the performance of the fund and the amount that can be invested. Remember, there is no guarantee that the value will be sufficient to repay the loan, but if the plan does well, it will be possible to pay off the mortgage early.

Many lenders are keen to ensure that funds accumulated in PEPs and ISAs remain relatively easy for borrowers to access. The advantage is that investors can withdraw funds after, say, a period of growth, and repay a proportion of their mortgage. However, this accessibility can be a disadvantage if money is withdrawn for other purposes, such as buying holidays or cars, so savings-linked mortgages like these are generally suitable only for disciplined savers.

*Pros and cons*

✔ PEPs and ISAs are tax free, although, unlike pension plans, contributions do not attract tax relief.

✔ These plans are highly flexible and funds can be accessed reasonably easily. For the undisciplined, this can be a disadvantage.

✔ Additional lump sum or regular contributions can be made.

✔ Investments can be targeted specifically at higher risk/higher reward assets, which may appeal to more speculative investors.

✘ There is a restriction on the amount that can be invested tax-efficiently each year. In practice this equates to about £580 per month (in 2005/6), so it is unlikely to be a problem for most people.

✘ Where funds are invested in higher risk assets, there is an increased chance that the proceeds of the plan will not match the amount of the mortgage at the time it is due to be repaid.

## Other repayment vehicles

There are many other investment plans that may potentially be used to repay a mortgage, such as unit trusts and schemes run by open-ended investment companies. However, these only really make sense if the borrower is utilizing his or her ISA allowance, as they are taxable versions of the same investments without the same ISA contribution limits.

Increasingly these days, borrowers are failing to link a repayment vehicle to their mortgage and are instead relying on an increase in value of the property to offset the loan, or upon a future event, such as an inheritance. This does not sit comfortably with some lenders, however, and as a general rule many prefer to see some plan to repay the loan.

It is worth repeating that for interest-only mortgages, the repayment vehicle is the instrument that will repay the loan, so it is vital to monitor its progress regularly. This will allow you stay on course to repay your mortgage when it is due or, as we hope, early.

# Chapter 4
# Other Mortgage Options

**Let's take** a closer look at some of the other types of mortgage available. There was a time for our parents when the mortgage interest rate was dictated by the bank and was more or less the same for all borrowers. Nowadays, there is a mind-boggling number of variations, from simple fixed rates to 'capped' and 'collared' loans and 'offset' accounts.

Before comparing the different rate types, it is worth taking a moment to think about the APR (annual percentage rate). Every company in the business of lending money or advancing credit is required by law to quote this rate. It is only one of a number of interest rates you will see quoted, and it is likely to be the highest.

Many mortgages are quoted at introductory interest rates that sound enticing. However, these fail to include the cost of arrangement fees and they won't immediately reflect any higher rate of interest that your borrowings will ultimately revert to. This is where APR comes in. It usually appears in brackets after the headline rate and is a representation of the total amount of interest that will be paid over the whole term of the loan, taking into account any special bonuses.

When comparing mortgages, particularly discounted rate mortgages, it is worth comparing the APR, especially when the offer seems too good to be true.

The following table is the kind of table you'll find in the national press, detailing the better rates. They will generally give you not only headline rates, but APRs and any catches or penalties that you may incur as part of the deal.

Interest rate comparisons:

| Lender | Type of mortgage | Period | Rate | Redemption |
|---|---|---|---|---|
| Bradford & Bingley | Fixed | To 31/12/2007 | 4.39% | To 31/12/2007 |
| Abbey | Capped | To 2/1/2011 | 4.99% | To 2/1/2011 |
| Portman Building Society | Variable with cash rebate | For term | 6.49% | First 5 years |

As illustrated in the table overleaf, changes in the interest rate can make a considerable difference to repayments, and almost all UK mortgages are subject to them at some point or other. Many of these rates can be traced back to changes in the underlying Bank of England base rate, which is effectively the interest rate at which the Bank of England lends to banks and other financial institutions, and which in turn impacts upon the interest rate that lenders offer mortgage borrowers.

The base rate is set at a level deemed to best match the target for overall inflation in the economy as determined by the Chancellor of the Exchequer, with a view to safeguarding the value of the currency both in the UK and abroad. In the past the base rate was set by politicians, but since 1997 it has been determined by the Bank of England Monetary Policy Committee (MPC). For the anoraks among us, the minutes of its monthly meeting, which are available on the Bank of England website (see page 186), provide a fascinating insight into the health of the UK economy.

The following table looks at the effect of interest rate changes on the monthly repayments of a capital and interest mortgage.

| The effect of interest rate changes on a £150,000 mortgage | |
| --- | --- |
| Interest rate | Monthly repayment |
| 4% | £ 800 |
| 5% | £ 887 |
| 6% | £ 978 |
| 7% | £ 1,073 |
| 8% | £ 1,171 |
| 9% | £ 1,273 |
| 10% | £ 1,377 |
| 11% | £ 1,484 |
| 12% | £ 1,594 |
| 13% | £ 1,705 |
| 14% | £ 1,819 |

Source: AWD plc

There are eight main interest rate options, and these are discussed in the following pages.

# 1. Variable rate mortgage

The variable rate, or standard variable rate as it is sometimes known, is the 'floating' mortgage rate set by the lender in relation to underlying economic conditions and commercial considerations. If you are not on a special interest rate, or have had the same mortgage for longer than, say, five years, it is likely that you are paying the lender's variable rate. Of our contributors, the Holleymans have a variable rate mortgage, and in their case they are paying interest only.

The economic conditions that affect the rate include the general investment climate, the rate of inflation and the Bank of England base rate, which dictates the rate at which the bank or building society can access money. The base rate is set each month by the Monetary Policy Committee, whose decisions are widely reported by the BBC and other national media.

Commercial considerations dictate the difference between the Bank of England rate and the lender's variable mortgage rate. Put simply, a bank or building society makes a profit by charging borrowers more in interest than it gives out to savers – how much more depends upon the respective interest rates charged or given. Thankfully, both savings and mortgages are competitive markets that offer plenty of consumer choice, so commercial pressures tend to keep rates keen. Among our contributors to the series, the MacVeans, the Casey-Pooles, and Heather and Chloe were aware of this, but have been constrained from changing their lender by redemption fees and penalties.

Standard variable rates have fluctuated widely and have been as high as 15.4% as recently as the 1990s. The following graph illustrates the recent history of the Halifax standard variable mortgage rate.

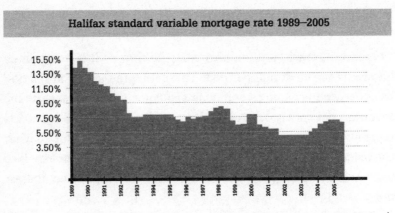

Source: www.moneyextra.co.uk

A disadvantage of variable rates is that your monthly mortgage payments will go up and down as rates change. When taking out a mortgage it is really important to remember that interest rates can increase significantly.

The graph below shows how a variable rate works in practice.

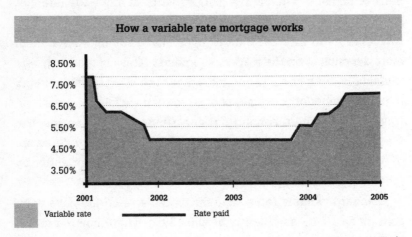

Source: AWD plc

## Pros and cons
✔ Easy to understand.
✘ If mortgage rates go up, so do your repayments.

## 2. Fixed rate mortgage

This type of mortgage guarantees to charge a known rate for a fixed period of time. Rates are usually available for periods of between two and five years. This type of mortgage is popular among our contributors; the MacVeans have a five-year fixed mortgage until September 2009, paying 5.99% and the Binners' mortgage is also fixed for five years at 5.15% until March 2007. Heather and Chloe have a slightly different arrangement in that £36,000 of their mortgage is fixed at 4.24% until March 2005 and £54,000 of it is fixed at 5.74% until October 2009.

Lenders generally charge an arrangement fee at the outset and levy an additional charge, known as a 'redemption penalty', if the mortgage is redeemed in full (or in part) within the fixed rate period. Many lenders extend this redemption penalty period beyond the end of the fixed term, stipulating that a borrower must remain with them on their variable rate for a while.

Redemption penalties are not a barrier to moving home, as most fixed rates can be 'moved' to another property, although penalties may apply if the amount of the mortgage is reduced if, for example, you move to a smaller property.

### CASE STUDY

Paddy and Mandy MacVean fixed their mortgage for five years so that they could budget more effectively. They know exactly what their monthly repayments are, and are unaffected by interest rate movements. However, there will be a redemption penalty amounting to around £5,500 if they want to move the mortgage.

Rates are largely dependent on the lender's judgement of the economic outlook for the years ahead. Fixed rate mortgages are therefore ideal for borrowers who wish to work to a known budget, as the mortgage cost is known in advance and guaranteed not to fluctuate during the fixed term. In cost terms, fixed rates can work for or against the borrower, as you are effectively second-guessing whether rates will rise or fall in the future.

If the variable rate rises above the level of the fixed rate, you will be better off than a borrower paying a variable rate. If rates fall, however, the borrower on the variable rate will be better off. This is illustrated by the graph below.

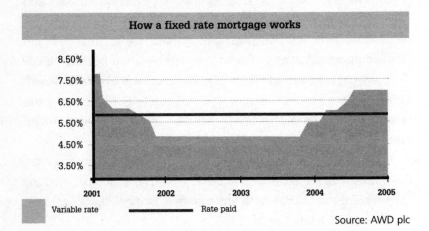

**How a fixed rate mortgage works**

Variable rate        Rate paid

Source: AWD plc

*Pros and cons*

✔ Monthly repayments are fixed.

✘ If interest rates go down, you end up paying more in relative terms.

**TOP TIP**

**Check out full redemption penalties in cash terms on any mortgage, and make sure you remember what they are. They can really hurt if you forget to take them into account when you move to a different provider.**

## 3. Capped and/or collared mortgage

A capped mortgage is based upon the variable rate but, as the name suggests, it has a limit placed upon the interest rate that you will pay, effectively capping it at a maximum level. A capped rate is arguably better than a fixed rate at the same level, as the borrower will benefit if the variable rate falls below the cap, and is protected from rate increases above the level of the cap (as is the fixed rate). This is illustrated in the graph below.

As with fixed rates, lenders will usually charge an arrangement fee at the outset, as well as a redemption penalty that may extend beyond the term of the capped rate.

It is common for lenders to offer a collared rate in conjunction with the capped rate, effectively a fixed point below which the rate cannot fall. For borrowers the cap and collar define the range at which mortgage interest can potentially be charged. Again, it is subject to the usual arrangement fees and redemption penalties.

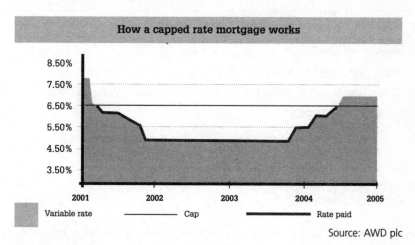

Source: AWD plc

### Pros and cons
✔ Keeps your repayments within known limits.
✗ Difficult to understand.

## 4. Cashback mortgage

This type of mortgage comes with a lump sum benefit for the borrower. On completion of the mortgage, the lender will issue a cheque to the borrower for a sum of around 3–6% of the amount borrowed, which can be used for any purpose. The actual amount depends upon the total amount borrowed compared to the value of the property (the loan to value ratio), and repayments are usually charged at the lender's standard variable rate.

Cashback mortgages are popular with first-time buyers, who may seek to replenish their emergency fund after using a large proportion of their savings to fund a deposit or home-purchase fees.

To prevent a borrower transferring to another lender and repeating the whole process, the lender will include a redemption penalty period, or require that the cashback is repaid if the mortgage is redeemed within a certain period. Of course, once the redemption penalty period runs out, the borrower is free to obtain another cashback mortgage with a different lender, subject to the costs associated with remortgaging.

*Pros and cons*
✔ You get 'free' money.
✘ You usually end up paying for your 'free' money with a slightly higher mortgage rate.

# 5. Discounted mortgage

To attract borrowers, many lenders offer discounted rates that are guaranteed to be below the standard variable rate by a stated percentage for a specific period. Discounted rates became popular in the 1990s and have almost entirely replaced variable rates for new borrowers – Duncan and Dan and Lucy both have discounted mortgages. As there is no element of risk, it makes sense for borrowers to choose a discounted rate and reduce their monthly payments rather than opt for the standard variable rate. One downside is that, as with a cashback mortgage, the lender is likely to apply a redemption penalty period, which may last beyond the term of the discount. The graph below illustrates how a discounted rate operates.

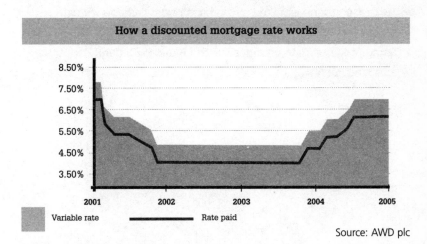

Source: AWD plc

## Pros and cons

✔ The initial mortgage rate is lower – and so are your monthly repayments.

✘ If you don't keep an eye on the rate, over time you can end up with an uncompetitive rate.

## 6. Tracker mortgage

This type of mortgage is designed to track the movement of an index, usually the Bank of England base rate. Most providers will guarantee to adjust borrowers' rates within a few days of any changes in the underlying base rate.

Standard variable rates (see page 77) are, of course, affected by changes in the base rate, but do not necessarily have an automatic link to them as tracker mortgages do.

It is important to compare one tracker rate against another, as sometimes there can be, albeit small, variances between organisations.

*Pros and cons*

✔ As the mortgage is linked to the base rate, you know exactly what rate you are paying.

✗ Some providers rate changes lag the Bank of England announcements.

## 7. Flexible mortgage

Unfortunately, flexible mortgages do not fit easily into a simple explanation. A relatively recent development in the mortgage market, they were introduced in response to a demand from borrowers for a more adaptable loan to match a more changeable career path. Julie has a flexible mortgage and is paying 0.75% above the Bank of England base rate for the life of her mortgage. Flexible mortgages can include provisions for some or all of the following features:

- Regular or irregular overpayments
- The ability to borrow back overpayments
- Payment holidays
- Pre-arranged further advances (often with a chequebook)
- A combination of fixed and variable rates
- A sympathetic redemption penalty structure to accommodate changing circumstances
- Sometimes the initial rate can be discounted to entice you into this sort of mortgage

*Pros and cons*
✔ You can move payments to suit your own circumstances.
✘ Sometimes you pay for the flexibility with a higher interest rate.

Research from the Council of Mortgage Lenders shows that the vast majority of people choose flexible mortgages because of the ease with which they allow the loan to be paid off early.

## 8. Offset and current account mortgages

With offset mortgages, your current account plus any savings accounts are held with the lender, and the balances of these are off-set against your outstanding mortgage. You effectively forgo interest on your accounts in order to reduce the amount you pay in mortgage interest. The theory is that this will allow you to repay your mortgage earlier. Savings are therefore a prerequisite for a mortgage of this type.

It is usually possible to link other debts, such as credit cards and personal loans, to the mortgage so that the interest is charged against these at the same rate as your mortgage, which is almost always considerably lower. Take care, though, that they are paid off in the same way as you would unconnected loans and credit cards, as there is a danger that short-term unsecured debts are simply converted into long-term mortgage debt. For this reason, offset and current account mortgages are generally suitable only for disciplined savers.

Current account mortgages go one stage further and lump all these accounts together so that you effectively operate one current account with a very, very large overdraft (the mortgage). Again, in practice, access to additional lump sums is reasonably easy (especially if a current account mortgage has been in operation for a period of years and some of the loan has been repaid), but a degree of borrower discipline is required to avoid the temptation to repeatedly increase the debt. Many lenders reduce this risk by restricting current account mortgages to borrowers with a high proportion of equity in their homes as opposed to, say, first-time buyers.

Offset or current account mortgages can be effective if, for example, you have large savings, an irregular income in a freelance capacity, or if your income consists of large bonuses. It is important to shop around, as flexibility comes at a price and the interest rate charged may not be as competitive as other variable rates. Lenders are also aware that you will be unlikely to transfer all your accounts subsequently to another lender because it will involve changing direct debit mandates, standing orders and payroll notifications, so they may take advantage of this by increasing the rate following an introductory period.

As with flexible mortgages, options such as payment holidays sound fantastic, but if you are serious about paying off your mortgage early (and let's face it – you bought this book, didn't you?), any missed payments simply serve to extend the amount of time that you are burdened with the debt.

*Pros and cons*
✔ Can save substantial amounts in interest.
✗ If you are not disciplined, you can end up with a longer-term mortgage – and pay more interest.

> '*If you would like to know the value of money, go and try to borrow some.*'
> Benjamin Franklin, American statesman and scientist (1706-90)

# Chapter 5
# You and Your Money

**There are some things** that we Brits find very difficult to discuss, even with our partners, and perhaps top of the list of uncomfortable topics is money. We'd rather jump off a cliff than reveal what's in our bank account.

> *'I have a perfectly fine relationship with money – I avoid it and it avoids me.'*
> Anonymous

## Your relationship with money

Some psychologists reckon that our attitudes to most aspects of life are determined by the age of six. Alongside that view is the nature/nurture debate, which can't decide whether those attitudes are formed by genetic inheritance or upbringing. Whatever the case, there can be little doubt that our parents influence us enormously, not least in our attitude to money.

I was brought up in a working-class household where one of the golden rules was 'You don't have what you can't afford to pay for'. Mortgages, credit cards and bank loans were just not the sort of things that my family would contemplate. What's more, those who had financial problems were dismissed as irresponsible, whatever the reason for their difficulties. At home money was always tight – to the extent that I never bothered to ask to go on school trips because I had the idea that my parents simply couldn't afford them. The frugal atmosphere meant that we always had to eat everything that was put in front of us, and the emphasis on being grateful for what I had when others hadn't has stayed with me for over 40 years.

In my case, being brought up with little money has made financial security very important to me, and dictates much of my attitude today. Most of my financial decisions are low risk, and I'm certainly a more conservative independent financial adviser than most because I hate losing money – mine or anyone else's. My upbringing pervades every bit of my life, and I imagine it will continue to do so until the day I die.

Understanding our attitude to money is fundamental to the financial strategies we choose. Recent studies suggest that those with an innate uninhibited perception of risk make the best fund managers because they are willing and able to take bigger bets than most of us. That may be true, but if I knew that a particular fund manager was making decisions like Mad Max, I would vote with my feet and take my hard-earned cash to another manager with an investment style and philosophy more in line with my own. This marrying up of philosophies is important – especially when it comes to mortgages.

To those of us with a conservative nature, paying off the mortgage is probably one of our primary financial aims in life. It might also mean that we will work harder to achieve it than someone who is more of a risk-taker. That type of person might prefer to take bigger bets on the stock market in order to make more money that can then be used to pay off the mortgage.

Your attitude to money can first manifest itself in the type of mortgage you choose. A conservative person might plump for a fixed rate mortgage on the basis that their monthly repayments are a known quantity and they can budget accordingly. This is what Paddy and Mandy MacVean have opted for. Another's view might be that interest rates are bound to fall, so they choose an index-tracking mortgage. Naturally, if they are wrong and interest rates go up, they could end up paying more than the person who opted for the fixed rate mortgage.

So attitudes to money and our relationship with it can vary from person to person. What happens, then, when two people living together have very different views about finances?

## CASE STUDIES

Of the contributors to the series, I felt that Sean and Anne-Marie Casey-Poole had the most significant gap in their attitudes to money. Sean was laissez-faire, almost casual about finances, whereas Anne-Marie was more conservative. In fact, the difference between them only came to light when it was revealed that Sean had more loans and debts than Anne-Marie knew about. He didn't regard his actions as deceitful or underhand; this was just the way he handled money, and he didn't see these additional loans and debts as an extra risk to their financial well-being. As a cautious person myself, who cannot bear to take out personal loans and run up credit card debts, I felt for Anne-Marie.

At the other end of the scale, I found Paddy and Mandy MacVean most in tune about money. They had been married for a long time, had raised a family, and had very similar views on religion and morality. There simply would not be much scope for disagreement: their attitudes had become subliminally aligned years ago. From a financial observer's standpoint, it was an enviable position to behold.

Simon and Debbie Binner were somewhere in the middle of these two extremes. Both enjoyed an affluent lifestyle and I felt they may be reluctant to give up their comforts in order to pay off the mortgage, even if the sacrifices were necessary for only two years. In fact, I felt this was a big enough issue to risk the couple's continuing participation in the whole experiment.

Heather and Chloe had started out with very different attitudes to money, but eventually reached common ground. When they first got together, Heather was heavily in debt but Chloe was reasonably solvent. They did the sensible thing – talked about how they could tackle the problem together, agreed a strategy and eventually paid off the debt. By living with a budget and tightening their belts, they got rid of a financial burden that was blighting their prospects for the future.

Lack of communication is not a problem with Dan and Lucy. They talk all the time, but rarely about money – it just doesn't interest them very much. However, with two growing boys, they know they have to improve their security, so they're making a real effort to be more financially aware.

The key task for couples who have conflicting views on financial matters is that they should discuss their attitudes to money in depth and explore the reasons behind them. Only by communicating will they have an understanding of the other's stance on financial issues.

Avoiding the subject simply allows the debt to grow and resentment to build up. Don't let it. Sit down together and draw up a financial plan, including how much each partner can contribute to the household budget, what remains and how much should be saved or spent.

According to Relate, the UK's largest provider of relationship counselling, money is the biggest cause of marital rows, especially for those on a low income. Money-related arguments are also more common if a couple have children under ten. More women than men initiate arguments over trust and secrecy issues related to money, whereas an equal proportion of men and women argue about the lack of money. Most arguments are caused by differing attitudes and spending priorities, and the easiest way to create a problem in a relationship is to avoid discussing the issue.

Your attitude to money can be plotted somewhere along the following scale:

←————————————————————————————————→

**'Having money provides me with security.'**                    **'Money is for enjoying you can't take it with you.'**

For most of us there is a happy medium somewhere in the middle, but does your partner agree with you? Like all things, finding the answer involves compromise, and it is important to agree limits, including how much you can each contribute towards paying off your mortgage every month.

It may be that money worries are masking a more serious and deep-rooted problem in your relationship. Do not despair: organizations such as Relate (see page 187) offer a range of support services that help all sorts of people to understand what is going on in their relationship and subsequently change things for the better.

## MONEY PROBLEMS

Answer the following questions to gauge how far money issues are coming between you and your partner. Place a tick in the appropriate box so that you can add up your score at the end.

1. **On pay day where does most of your money go?**
a. Your savings account ❑
b. A joint 'household' account ❑
c. To pay off your credit cards ❑

2. **Which of the following best resembles your investment portfolio?**
a. Some unit trusts and shares, a pension and a healthy savings account ❑
b. A small emergency fund (up to three months' gross salary) ❑
c. £150 in a building society account and a premium bond ❑

3. **What best describes your attitude to money?**
a. Savings provide security: I save some of all I earn ❑
b. I save when I can, but it is not the be-all and end-all ❑
c. Money is for spending; savings are just numbers ❑

4. **What best describes your partner's attitude to money?**
a. Savings provide security: I save some of all I earn ❑
b. I save when I can, but it is not the be-all and end-all ❑
c. Money is for spending; savings are just numbers ❑

5. **How often do you and your partner disagree over money?**
a. Never or rarely ❑
b. Sometimes ❑
c. Often ❑

**6. You splash out on a luxury item – how do you feel?**

a. You can't wait to go home and show it to your partner ❑

b. A bit guilty, it's expensive but you deserve it ❑

c. Concerned, but if you hide the receipt, you can pretend
it was in the sale ❑

**7. Do you have an emergency fund?**

a. Yes, more than three months' gross salary ❑

b. Yes, up to three months' gross salary ❑

c. Yes – quite a few pound coins in a jam jar ❑

**8. What do you do when a bill arrives?**

a. File it: all my bills are paid by direct debit ❑

b. Pay it straight away ❑

c. Wait until pay day and see how much is left,
or ignore it until the reminder arrives ❑

**9. How many credit cards do you have?**

a. None ❑

b. One ❑

c. Two or more ❑

**10. Do you have a joint account?**

a. Yes, all our bills are paid from it by direct debit ❑

b. Yes, but we don't use it much ❑

c. No ❑

**11. How often do you clear the balance on your credit card(s)?**

a. Always/I don't have a credit card ❑

b. Usually; only large purchases such as holidays
are spread ❑

c. Occasionally ❑

**12. What would you do with a £5,000 lottery win?**

a.    Put it all into investments ❏

b.    Pay off the credit cards and spend the rest ❏

c.    Spend it all – it's a windfall ❏

Now add up your score:

**a.** = 3 points; **b.** = 2 points; **c.** = 1 point

# How did you do?

Compare your results. If you and your partner have similar scores, you share the same attitude towards money. You may still need to take action occasionally, but money is probably not an area of conflict. The wider the gap between your scores, the more you have to sort out.

## 12–22 points

Oh, dear – you're like Sean and Anne-Marie. It's likely that money is a major source of conflict between you and your partner, but don't worry – confront the problem head-on and you should be able to whip your finances into shape. Take time to sit down together and plan your budget (see page 118).

If you don't already have a joint current account, consider opening one. You could also open a joint savings account that requires two signatures to access. Arrange for a set amount to be transferred into these accounts every month to cover your major bills and to begin to accumulate a buffer. If you are running high credit card balances, get the scissors to your cards. If your debts seem unmanageable, swallow your pride and contact the companies to whom you owe money: they'd rather negotiate a repayment plan with you than have their letters ignored.

Make a list of what needs doing, divide the jobs up between

you and discuss progress every day. If you need to regain control of your finances, make a proper plan and make sure you implement it quickly. Take a morning off work to make arrangements to fully discuss your financial views and future, if you have to. You will find that life is easier and much more fun when you are in control of your finances.

## 23–29 points

Like Arthur and Mary, you're almost there, but could do better. Finances probably aren't the cause of all your disagreements, but shopping trips can sometimes be a bit tense. Review your finances and see if you can reach a compromise, perhaps by making a small increase in the amount that you save each month. If you're not saving, now's the time to begin saving a regular monthly amount. A good way of keeping on top of household bills is to ensure they're paid by direct debit from a joint account. Remember to make provision for treats or future holidays, and try to agree some further financial steps, such as opening another savings account or investigating a remortgage or a pension.

Remember to keep a regular eye on your finances. When is the last time you checked to see how competitive your mortgage or savings rate is?

## 30 points and above

Congratulations! Like Heather and Chloe, you've got your finances well under control and are ideally placed to begin paying off your mortgage early. You're probably well positioned for most eventualities, and it is unlikely that money is causing any problems in your relationship. Do not be complacent, however. Longer-term financial planning considerations should come to the fore, especially if you have dependants.

As well as maximizing opportunities to pay off your mortgage, you should ensure that any investments are held in a diversified portfolio of asset classes rather than concentrated in a few sectors or, worse still, the shares of only a few companies. It is worth considering having your finances reviewed by an investment professional, who can then be retained to provide ongoing advice and draw your attention to any new products that might be of interest to you. Not all independent financial advisers are hungry for commission, especially if they work for a company that offers a fee-based service (something that all professional firms should offer). Even if you are maximizing mortgage repayments, it is worth considering an equity portfolio that can potentially increase in value at a rate much higher than the interest you will save by repaying the mortgage, and in the long term help you to repay the loan even more quickly.

## TOP TIP

**Do a budget (see page 118). If you don't know where you are now, you will never know where you need to get to.**

## FOCUS ON FINANCES

Here are some tips that can help you to sort out your money problems:

- Be realistic about ideas.
- How many ideas can you cope with?
- Rule ideas in or out as quickly as possible.
- Be focused.
- Do the numbers.

## Your attitude to risk

There is some element of risk inherent in all financial transactions. Having a clear idea of your personal attitude to risk is vital in determining the correct approach for you to repay your mortgage. There would be little sense in pursuing an aggressive investment strategy if it stopped you from sleeping at night, or, worse still, if you lost money that you simply could not afford to lose.

Put simply, the greater the risk, the greater the potential for capital gain or loss. Sometimes it can be better understood by an analysis of the past, although there can be no certainty that events of the past will repeat themselves in the future.

Important factors that must be taken into account include your age, state of health, marital status, dependants, career aspirations, current investments and income requirements. In addition, the type of mortgage you have, the remaining term and the balance of the loan outstanding are also important considerations.

As you get older, you may find yourself becoming less tolerant of risk. 'Lifestyle events', such as marriage and childbirth, can bring about changes in risk tolerance overnight. Assessing a suitable level of risk is not simply a matter of picking a number on a scale of 1–10.

### CASE STUDY

When the series began, Sean and Anne-Marie were in desperate need of some budgeting, but they have conflicting attitudes towards money. Sean describes himself as reckless; Anne-Marie is much more cautious. She once lost 44 kg (7 stone) in ten months, which proves that she has will power and self-discipline. This augurs well for the future. If she can discipline both of them to the same extent, I suspect budgeting could save them a huge amount of money.

# KNOW YOUR RISK PROFILE

What type of investor are you? Check out the categories below before embarking on any investment or savings strategy.

## Total risk intolerance

- No investment risk whatsoever can be accepted.

## Cautious risk profile

- Relatively low growth expectations and limited tolerance of capital losses.
- Aiming to protect capital against the effects of inflation over the medium to longer term.
- Acceptance of asset diversification into shares and fixed-interest securities alongside and in place of cash.
- Some inaccessibility to capital may be tolerated.

## Balanced risk profile

- Acceptance of the possibility of reducing values over the shorter term in return for the expectation of greater returns over the longer term.
- A moderate tolerance of capital losses.
- Aiming to increase capital over the medium to longer term.
- Expectation of asset diversification into shares and fixed-interest securities alongside and in place of cash.
- Some inaccessibility to capital may be tolerated.

## Speculative risk profile

- Tolerance of the possibility of sharply reducing values in the shorter term in return for the expectation of significantly greater returns over the longer term.
- A strong tolerance of capital losses.

- Can afford to accept considerable fluctuations in value and uncertain investment returns.
- Unconcerned about inflation.
- Requirement for broadly spread allocation covering most asset classes.
- Acceptance that higher-risk investments may not always be easily realized.

## Celebrate even the small successes

There is nothing like the **feeling of success** to fuel further success. **Build achievable milestones** into your overall plan, and **celebrate as you hit each one.**

## Which strategy is best for you?

If you are serious about paying off your mortgage early, you must decide on a strategy and agree it with your partner. To decide which is the best strategy, you first need to take stock of where you are.

If you have five years remaining on your mortgage and owe £5,000, paying off your mortgage in two years could be a very achievable goal. If, however, you have just taken out a £150,000 mortgage over 25 years, you may need to broaden your time horizons or pin your hopes on the Lottery.

If you already have a mortgage with at least two or more years remaining, it makes sense to begin by looking at your existing deal. You can probably save some money, and thus begin paying off your mortgage early, by changing your mortgage to one with a lower interest rate. Of course, it is not enough simply to remortgage and decrease your repayments. You will need to maintain your payments or increase them as much as possible so that you can make serious inroads into the capital you have borrowed and pay off your mortgage more quickly.

Ask your existing lender what offers are available to you and compare these with the deals offered by other lenders. Don't simply walk into the next bank or building society on the high street: check out best buy deals at websites such as Moneyextra (see page 187), or speak to an independent financial adviser. It should be possible to achieve a healthy saving on your monthly repayments that will translate into weeks, months or years off your mortgage.

Make sure that your current mortgage does not include heavy penalties for transferring. You should be OK if it has been running for, say, five years or more, but it is worth double-checking anyway. Your current lender will give you a mortgage redemption statement on request, which should detail the exact amount outstanding, as well as any penalties. If you remortgage, you are likely to incur costs, so make sure your new deal remains attractive even after these have been accounted for. You may be faced with an arrangement fee, a valuation fee and legal fees, all of which can add up to £1,000 or more. With some deals, these costs are paid by the lender. Whatever the case, it is important to understand how much your new deal will cost you in total so that you do not receive any unpleasant surprises.

## CASE STUDY

Julie is particularly keen to remortgage her house because this strategy is within her comfort zone and it will release some equity. With this she wants to buy a development property abroad (she favours Turkey) to rent out or sell. If she could buy for, say, £65,000, then sell for £100,000, she could clear £35,000 and pay off a fair wad of her mortgage. Sounds great in theory, especially as global property prices have risen over the last few years. But it's all too easy to fall into the trap of believing that prices can only go up. Julie must also remember that she's on a two-year timescale. If she enters the property market for what turns out to be the wrong two years and loses money, it will be a severe setback. To me, this plan sounds like a quick fix that Julie hasn't really thought through. She has done no in-depth research and is relying on hearsay about the benefits of such a strategy.

If you have a competitive mortgage and your monthly repayments come down due to a cut in interest rates (as they did in August 2005 when the Bank of England Monetary Policy Committee cut the rate by 0.25%), don't congratulate yourself that you are a few quid better off each month. Tell your lender that you would like to maintain the level of your repayments (you could afford them without problem last month, couldn't you?), and have the excess payment set against the outstanding capital. Or, better still, increase your repayments and begin to make a real difference.

If you have, say, ten years or more left on your mortgage, don't worry, the magic of compound interest can really work in your favour and some huge savings may be achieved. Work through the budget planner on page 118 and see where you can shave some costs. It might mean eating more supermarket brand food for a while, but imagine how nice it will be when you have paid off your mortgage. You will be able to take a few more holidays and do what you want when you want.

Remember that your mortgage is likely to be your cheapest form of borrowing, so try to wipe out any other form of borrowing, such as personal loans or credit cards, before looking to pay more off your mortgage. There is no point paying off a loan on which you are being charged 5% interest if you have a £1,000 credit card debt incurring interest charges of 15% or more. Get rid of the most expensive borrowing first.

## CASE STUDY

Mary and Arthur Holleyman were in just this position when I first met them. Apart from their mortgage commitments, they had four other debts totalling £19,350 that were attracting hefty amounts of interest:

| | |
|---|---|
| RAC loan | £8,500 |
| Tesco Visa | £3,000 |
| Halifax Visa | £7,500 |
| Current account overdraft | £350 |

Before we could tackle the mortgage loans, we would have to manage these additional debts effectively. This was the plan:

- Sell second car for around £7,000 to pay off most of the RAC loan.
- Use the £375 per month saved to start repaying the two Visa cards.
- Swap Tesco Visa to Marbles, which offered 0% interest for nine months.
- Once the interest-free period ends on the Halifax Visa, look for another 0% interest-free deal with another credit card provider.

### TOP TIP

The 0% interest-free rate on credit cards is extremely important if you are not going to pay them off month by month. This means that the entirety of any amount you do pay off is deducted from the capital amount, rather than part of it going to reduce the interest you owe. Efficient management of debt can save thousands of pounds a year.

# Get your ducks in a row

More than anything else, being organized is the best help in dealing with finances. For most people, lifestyle is dictated by income. Consider when you have had a pay rise in the past: did you find yourself with spare money at the end of the month? Or when interest rates changed, did you notice that you were suddenly £25 per month better or worse off? Probably not.

This is Parkinson's Law in action. That law states: 'Work expands so as to fill the time available for its completion.' Similarly, our lifestyle adapts quickly and subtly to our circumstances, expanding or contracting according to our income. Could you survive happily on £100 per month less? Quite possibly, especially when you consider that a large proportion of our disposable income is spent on 'leisure'. That's why it's not a good idea to try to accumulate savings in a current account – if the money is accessible, it's all too easy to spend it.

Most organized savers will arrange for an amount to be transferred regularly from their current accounts into a separate, less accessible account as soon as possible after they receive it – often the day after pay day. Don't wait until the end of the month when the funds are less likely to be available.

Creating the mindset that savings are untouchable is one of the secrets of success. None of our contributors had this attitude, so life was proving to be immensely costly for them.

What is clear is that with a little effort and imagination it is easy to pay off your mortgage early and become a fully debt-free home owner. And, who knows, in a couple of years you could be planning that mortgage-burning party to celebrate your financial freedom.

## Bite-sized chunks

*René says*

Once you have worked out exactly how much you will need to find to pay off your mortgage early and decided how long you will give yourself to achieve this, produce **monthly and quarterly targets**. Many small targets are much easier to hit than one colossal target set way off in the future.

## Amour bon marché

For those who are determined to pay off their mortgage early and are seriously economizing, here are some low-budget ideas:

- Run a hot bath with lots of bubbles to relax.
- Spend an evening dancing to your favourite songs.
- Drag the duvet on to the sofa, close the curtains and snuggle up in front of your favourite film.
- Cook a meal for two and share it bistro-style, complete with candles, freshly picked flowers and a bottle of cheap plonk.

*'We all have the means to become prosperous, we just have to find the balance between our wealth and our needs'*

Robert Bourassa, Premier of Quebec 1970-76,1986-94

## TIPS TO BOOST YOUR INCOME

• Get a second job or take in a lodger.

• If you have a little capital and some drive and ambition, think about starting your own business, like the people involved in the series. This really can lead to paying off the mortgage early, and possibly in two years or less.

• Develop your idea as far as possible without incurring too many costs. Your local Council should be able to point you in the direction of a business club or support service, such as Business Link. Here, at little or no cost, you can get professional assistance to develop your ideas, which will significantly increase your chances of success. If your business takes off you will soon be looking for ways to invest your money, safe in the knowledge that your home is paid for.

• Make sure you do not stretch yourself too far. You don't want to direct so much of your money to repaying your mortgage that you create a cash-flow problem when unexpected costs arise.

• Try to keep three months' income in an emergency fund. If you don't, you may end up paying overdraft and bank charges if you run out of your own money.

• Don't redirect cash that is needed for other necessities. There is no point incurring a large fine by not paying for the television licence or being pursued through the courts for unpaid utility bills.

- If you have some investments, consider how hard they are working for you and whether they might be better employed to reduce your mortgage.

- A relatively small overpayment can lead to a huge saving in total mortgage interest throughout the term of the loan. If you can afford to, you might choose to speculate a little with your investments in an attempt to make a profit and repay your mortgage early. Be careful if you follow this strategy. To be successful, you will need to target fairly aggressive returns to outstrip your mortgage rate, which itself will be higher than the interest rate paid to savers.

- With higher potential rewards comes higher risk and the increased likelihood that any speculative investment will lose rather than gain money.

- Don't overlook saving for your retirement.

- Try auctioning unwanted items on an internet auction site such as Ebay. This money-making idea does not require any initial outlay and can be a fun way of making some serious money.

- Check you are getting the best deal on all insurances, from life insurance, to building and health insurance.

- Look into switching your utility supplier by looking at competitor's deals. You could save hundreds of pounds a year.

# Chapter 6
# Getting a Grip on Your Mortgage

**As we touched** on earlier, there can be many reasons to pay off your mortgage early, but none quite as compelling as simply the money you save by doing so. For most of us, our home is the by far the largest purchase that we will ever make, and the sums involved are truly staggering. We tend to think of the cost of our homes as the purchase price that we pay for them or the amount of our monthly repayments. However when we get around to calculating the actual cost, we wonder how it is possible for anybody but a millionaire to afford it.

## Understanding interest

To understand the effect of paying interest, let's use the example of a £150,000 capital and interest repayment mortgage at an average interest rate of 6% over 25 years. Excluding fees and any set-up charges, the total amount that you will repay to the bank or building society is £289,950. If the average interest rate is increased to 7% or 8%, this total rises to £318,031 and £347,433 respectively – over a third of a million pounds to purchase a property below the average UK value.

> *'Debt is like any other trap, easy enough to get into, but hard enough to get out of'*
> Henry Wheeler Shaw, American humourist

## CASE STUDY

Heather and Chloe's mortgage is £90,000. Assuming the current interest rate stays the same, if they continued with their mortgage to term they would pay a total of £76,362 in interest, but if they manage to repay their mortgage in two years, their total savings in terms of mortgage repayments could be as much as £166,362 when interest is added on to the capital.

There are some tactics that can be easily employed at a modest extra cost (financial and personal) to knock years off your mortgage and save you pounds. But first it is worth taking some time to understand the figures involved and how they build up. And to do this you need to understand compound interest.

René says

### It's not all pain

Paying off your mortgage need not be a painful and distressing experience. When things do become difficult (as they will from time to time) remind yourself why you are doing this. Keep that vision of a mortgage-free life clear in your mind and write it down to keep yourself inspired. This could be a life-changing experience – enjoy it!

> *'The most powerful force in the
> universe is compound interest.'*
> Albert Einstein, German-born physicist (1879–1955)

## How compound interest works

If you have savings, compound interest works in your favour
because it pays interest on the interest earned. If you have borrowings, such as a mortgage, compound interest works against you,
charging you interest on interest, and could almost double your
original loan. This is why banks and building societies are so keen
to give out mortgages – they make huge amounts of money from
our borrowing. It's also why the interest rate is such an important
part of the equation, even though it is one of the smallest numbers
you will see when discussing your mortgage.

The interest that you pay is just the charge for borrowing money.
You may think that if you borrow £150,000 at an interest rate of 6%,
you will pay £9,000 in interest charges – after all 150,000 x 6% =
£9,000. In fact, on a capital and interest repayment mortgage at an
average interest rate of 6% over 25 years (excluding fees and any
set-up charges) the total amount that you will eventually pay in
interest charges alone will be more like £140,000.

This is because the interest is calculated each month based
upon the entire outstanding balance. Let's take another look at
the projected repayments based upon a capital and interest mortgage of £150,000 borrowed at a fixed rate of 6% over 25 years
(see page 42).

| | | Schedule of repayments on a capital and interest mortgage | | | |
|---|---|---|---|---|---|
| year | balance at 1 January | annual payment | capital repaid | interest | balance 31 December |
| 1 | £150,000 | £11,734 | £2,734 | £9,000 | £147,266 |
| 2 | £147,266 | £11,734 | £2,898 | £8,836 | £144,368 |
| 3 | £144,368 | £11,734 | £3,072 | £8,662 | £141,296 |
| 4 | £141,296 | £11,734 | £3,256 | £8,478 | £138,040 |
| 5 | £138,040 | £11,734 | £3,452 | £8,282 | £134,588 |
| 10 | £118,583 | £11,734 | £4,619 | £7,115 | £113,964 |
| 15 | £92,545 | £11,734 | £6,181 | £5,553 | £86,363 |
| 20 | £57,700 | £11,734 | £8,272 | £3,462 | £49,428 |
| 21 | £49,428 | £11,734 | £8,768 | £2,966 | £40,660 |
| 22 | £40,660 | £11,734 | £9,294 | £2,440 | £31,365 |
| 23 | £31,365 | £11,734 | £9,852 | £1,882 | £21,513 |
| 24 | £21,513 | £11,734 | £10,443 | £1,291 | £11,070 |
| 25 | £11,070 | £11,734 | £11,070 | £664 | £0 |

Source: AWD plc

To appreciate the effect of compound interest, you need only look at the totals for the first five years. After five years you will have paid a whopping £43,258 in interest, but only £15,412 in capital repayments. Depressing, isn't it?

The reason that Einstein considered compound interest to be man's greatest invention is the positive effect that it can have on savings. Einstein is credited with discovering the 'rule of 72', which is used to determine how long it will take to double your money at any given interest rate. The mathematics is simple, as demonstrated by the example on page 112.

**If you invest £1,000 at 6% interest, how long will it take to double your money?**
Simply divide the number 72 by the interest rate:
72 ÷ 6 = 12.

At an interest rate of 6%, it will take 12 years to double your money to £2,000.

It will take nine years at 8% interest (72 ÷ 8 = 9),
six years at 12% interest (72 ÷ 12 = 6), and so on.

Now consider the effect of doubling your money many times, and it is easy to see the power of compound interest: £10,000 ... £20,000 ... £40,000 ... £80,000 ... £160,000 ...

The trick is to ensure that you double your savings as many times as possible. At the current level of interest rates, the message is clear. For most people it takes a very, very long time to save enough money in a bank or building society to make a significant dent in a big mortgage.

## Ways of paying less

### Reduce the term and your costs by paying a little extra

Where your mortgage is concerned, compound interest is not all bad news, as there are ways to get a better deal. One is to reduce the term of the loan. You will recall that, excluding fees and set-up costs, the total charge for a £150,000 capital and interest repayment mortgage at 6% over 25 years is £289,950.

If, however, you are able to reduce the term of the loan, some huge savings are available. The same £150,000 mortgage at 6% repaid over a term of 20 years will cost approximately £32,000 less, whereas with a 15-year term, the saving equates to more than £62,000. So even if our experiment shows that a mortgage can't be paid off in two years, reducing the term of the mortgage results in a huge saving.

Of course, your monthly repayments must increase in order to repay the amount borrowed in a shorter period of time, but these figures represent the saving that you will achieve even accounting for the increased monthly cost. Taking our £150,000 mortgage at an interest rate of 6%, the cost difference between repayments over 25 years and over 20 years is about £110 per month, considerably less than the daily cost of a packet of cigarettes. Remember, by paying just £110 per month more, your total repayments are reduced by nearly £32,000. If you are able to afford an extra £200 per month, the term could be reduced from 25 years to 18 years and 3 months, and the saving increases to more than £48,000 – potentially more if interest rates are higher. An extra £300 per month will bring the term of the mortgage down to 15 years and save £62,300 in repayments.

These figures are the amount of money that you will save in pounds and pence by increasing your capital and interest mortgage repayments. Don't despair if you have an interest-only mortgage – most lenders will allow additional repayments of capital each month, which will have the same effect.

## Remortgage your way to financial freedom

What if you simply can't stretch to paying a bit extra every month? In that case, you can make your existing repayments work harder by obtaining a better rate. This could be the equivalent of paying additional hundreds of pounds per month, depending on the size of your mortgage. Better rates can sometimes be obtained either with your existing lender or by shopping around for the best deal. What most lenders fail to advertise is that they offer lower rates to new borrowers, while loyal customers who have been with them for any length of time pay a higher variable rate. Not all is lost, however, as many lenders will make new borrower rates available to existing customers if you ask. So try it – there's nothing to lose.

It is usually possible to move on to a new rate every 3–5 years, although it is really important to be aware of redemption penalty clauses as they can be a sharp and expensive sting in the tail of your mortgage. If you are in a penalty period, check when it expires, as it may be beneficial to wait and take action without penalty.

## Consolidate personal debt

Another way of saving money is to consolidate personal debts and add them to your mortgage. Credit cards, store cards and personal loans are all calculated with reference to interest rates that are considerably higher than mortgage rates, often with an APR of up to 30%. Consolidation can be an effective strategy, but you should take care not to rely upon converting short-term borrowing to long-term debt on a regular basis.

## TOP THREE REASONS FOR DEBT PROBLEMS

- Sudden change in personal circumstances, typically from job loss, relationship breakdown or illness.
- Low income – the consequences of living for a long time on very little money.
- Overcommitment – too many loans that cannot be repaid promptly.

## CASE STUDY

Unusually for an accountant, Julie has built up a debt on her credit cards of around £15,000 while having around £9,000 in a savings account. This just doesn't make sense. She might pay around 18% a year or more in interest rate charges, but will be lucky to get 5% a year in interest on her savings – and that's before tax. On £6,000, for example, that's over £1,080 in charges and around £200 in interest – a difference of over £800 to her disadvantage.

This is an important lesson for all of us. If you have debts on credit cards or personal loans but also have money in a savings account, it is generally better to pay off your debts. The savings on what might seem like relatively small debts can be huge. Even if you don't have savings in a bank or building society account, you should regularly check your credit cards, personal loans and mortgage to make sure that you are getting the best possible rate.

### DID YOU KNOW?

Britain's personal debt is increasing at a rate of £1 million every four minutes and currently totals more than £1 trillion.

Source: Credit Action

## Move house

Information from the 2005 British Household Panel Survey suggests that the average length of time people remain in the same home is between five and ten years. Surprisingly, one in six moves is from owner occupation to the private rented sector. This can be accounted for by a number of factors, including elderly people moving into sheltered accommodation, moves resulting from repossessions and moves for job reasons. On the whole, renting property tends to be short term, and one in three renters who moves becomes an owner-occupier.

Moving house is often the prompt that encourages people to reconsider the structure of their mortgage. Many will seek to borrow more, perhaps because their earnings have increased and they want to go up the property ladder. Others may be consolidating debt or moving to a smaller property, either to reduce monthly outgoings or to use the equity that has accumulated in their home. Whatever the reason, borrowers should always take the opportunity to shop around and see if they can improve their mortgage deal.

Moving is also the ideal opportunity to alter the timescale of your mortgage. If you have 15 years remaining on your mortgage but can afford additional repayments, it is worth considering reducing the loan to, say, ten or 12 years.

Most mortgages can be transferred to your new property (in mortgage jargon they are 'portable'), although there may be penalties if you borrow less than the original mortgage. If you move house and downsize to a smaller house, you can always use some or all of the profit on the larger house to pay off some of your mortgage.

Both remortgaging and moving house begin with what can seem to be a mountain of paperwork, not to mention the costs. Solicitors, stamp duty, estate agent fees, redecorating – it all adds up. It's not as daunting as it looks, though, especially if you are organized and have easy access to pay slips, bank statements and P60s. The whole process can still take eight weeks or so, and may involve a visit from a valuer (a surveyor or estate agent that the lender will send to confirm the value of the property), but when you balance any inconvenience against the potential savings, it is no contest. If you engage an adviser or intermediary, he or she should be able to steer you through the paperwork quickly and answer any questions you may have.

## Not too much

Do not attempt **too many initiatives** in one go. To try too many things simultaneously is to risk doing them all badly. Ask yourself which one or two of the approaches **is most likely** to work and which will make the biggest dent in your mortgage.

## Budgeting

If you are serious about paying off your mortgage early, budgeting is essential. This doesn't mean that you need to live off cold baked beans for the next five years. Many of our contributors have taken their budgets to heart, and they are the ones who will also make the biggest savings.

There is an old saying that if you watch the pennies, the pounds will look after themselves. In fact, it is remarkable how much can be saved (and put towards repaying the mortgage) by simply making a few economies. There's no need to become tight-fisted, avoid buying your round or alienate your friends. All you have to do is shop smarter.

# HOW TO DRAW UP A HOUSEHOLD BUDGET

Get all your paperwork together – bills, bank statements, mortgage details, etc. – and sort it into piles. Put some music on, open a (cheap) bottle of wine and get some pencils. Using the chart below, list all your regular incomings, then all your regular outgoings.

## BUDGET PLANNER

### INCOME

| | |
|---|---|
| Net salary | £ |
| Interest from savings/ dividends | £ |
| Other income | £ |
| **Total** | **£** |

### HOUSEHOLD EXPENDITURE

| | |
|---|---|
| Mortgage or rent | £ |
| Home telephone | £ |
| Mobile telephone | £ |
| Electricity | £ |
| Gas | £ |
| Water | £ |
| Maintenance / repairs | £ |
| Television licence | £ |
| Other | £ |
| **Total** | **£** |

## TRANSPORT

| | |
|---|---|
| Buses / taxis / trains | £ |
| Car payment (if applicable) | £ |
| Insurance | £ |
| Tax | £ |
| Fuel | £ |
| Maintenance / repairs | £ |
| Parking | £ |
| Other | £ |
| **Total** | **£** |

## INSURANCE

| | |
|---|---|
| Buildings insurance | £ |
| Home contents insurance | £ |
| Medical insurance | £ |
| Life cover | £ |
| Travel insurance | £ |
| Endowment | £ |
| Other | £ |
| **Total** | **£** |

## LOANS, SAVINGS AND INVESTMENTS

| | |
|---|---|
| Personal loan | £ |
| Student loan | £ |
| Credit card(s) | £ |
| Pension | £ |
| Individual savings account (ISA) | £ |
| Investment account | £ |
| Child savings | £ |
| Other | £ |
| **Total** | **£** |

## FOOD

| | |
|---|---|
| Groceries | £ |
| Eating out / takeaways | £ |
| Other | £ |
| **Total** | **£** |

## FAMILY

| | |
|---|---|
| Clothes (schoolwear / sports equipment) | £ |
| School fees / tuition | £ |
| School supplies | £ |
| Lunch money | £ |
| Child care | £ |
| Toys / games | £ |
| Other | £ |
| **Total** | **£** |

## HOLIDAY

| | |
|---|---|
| Holiday package | £ |
| Flights | £ |
| Hotels | £ |
| Spending money | £ |
| Other | £ |
| **Total** | **£** |

## PERSONAL

| | |
|---|---|
| Hair / nails | £ |
| Clothing | £ |
| Dry cleaning | £ |
| Health club | £ |
| Other | £ |
| **Total** | **£** |

## ENTERTAINMENT

| | |
|---|---|
| Satellite television | £ |
| Internet | £ |
| Books | £ |
| Videos / DVDs | £ |
| CDs | £ |
| Cinema / theatre / concerts | £ |
| Sporting events | £ |
| Clubs | £ |
| Magazines | £ |
| Newspapers | £ |
| **Total** | **£** |

| | |
|---|---|
| **TOTAL NET INCOME** | **£** |
| **TOTAL OUTGOINGS** | **£** |
| **NET DISPOSABLE INCOME** | **£** |

### TOP TIP

**A fixed rate mortgage helps enormously with budgeting because you know exactly what your monthly repayments are and they are unaffected by interest rate movements.**

When you've done this exercise you can see exactly what you have left at the end of the month (your net disposable income). The next step is to focus on how you can improve the figures. Try to concentrate on achievable short-term goals, such as reducing the grocery bill, rather than larger aims, such as getting rid of your mortgage. If you set your mind to it, you'll find that you can quickly achieve targets that both you and your partner are aiming for.

We all know that just when we are getting on top of things, the boiler/television/car/washing machine will break down and present us with an unforeseen cost. A little forward planning for such eventualities will make life a lot easier, so build a contingency fund into your savings.

## CASE STUDY

Sean and Anne-Marie had never itemized what they spend over the course of a month. The result shocked them to the core. This is an important lesson. In order to know where and what you spend, write down your day-to-day expenditure for one month. Don't cheat – include everything. You'll be surprised if you have never done it before. Once you've got over the shock, the next thing to do is to decide what you can cut back on, and prepare a proper budget.

## TOP TIP

We all go through times when lots of extra bills and expenses arise. Nonetheless, you really need to know how much you spend each month. It's not difficult. You just need to keep all your receipts for, say, three months, and work out the average. Remember to include a quarter of annual payments for outgoings such as insurance and the TV licence. You'll be surprised how much you fritter away on eating out, coffees and socializing.

## CASE STUDIES

Our contributors found all sorts of ways to save money. Arthur sold his beloved boat, while Mary took to using a bicycle and left the car at home. She also sorted through her vast wardrobe and sold off several hundreds of pounds' worth of clothes. Lucy hopped on her bike and went into the countryside to pick nettles for making soup. At different times she also scoured the hedgerows for berries and nuts. Meanwhile, Sean spent less on socializing, which benefited his waistline as much as his bank balance. Paddy and Mandy saved £221 per month by cancelling standing orders and direct debits, and in the process brought their bank charges down by £60. Look hard enough and you too can find relatively painless ways of budgeting.

### Smart shopping

If you are prepared to wait for a couple of days, almost anything can be bought cheaper off the Internet, the general rule being that the more expensive the item, the bigger the saving to be made. However, big savings are also available on relatively inexpensive items, such as CDs. The latest chart entry, for example, will cost around £12–£15 in a music store, £10–£12 in a supermarket and perhaps £7 from a dedicated Internet site. Security concerns about online shopping have reduced in recent years, and in many cases you'll find your bargain at the online branch of the high street music store where you began your search.

There are a number of dedicated price comparison websites, such as Kelkoo, which, once you have entered the name and model of the product you require, will scour the Internet to find you the cheapest site to purchase it from.

## CASE STUDY

Arthur and Mary cut back hard on their socializing, and missed the tipple they used to enjoy. What did they do? They collected coupons from Tesco and eventually redeemed them for a case of cheap red wine, which they eked out in front of the television. They'd never enjoyed their drinks so much!

## Cutting back on luxuries

Consider how much money you could save by giving up a few luxuries. For example, if you gave up a monthly subscription to Sky TV and put the £33 per month against your mortgage repayments, this could save £19,333 when set against the cost of the capital and interest of a £150,000 mortgage over 25 years.

When translated into total savings, based upon our £150,000 capital and interest repayment mortgage, the full cost of luxuries over the term of a 25-year mortgage can be eye-opening. For example, by giving up these luxuries you would save the following amounts against a 25-year mortgage:

| | |
|---|---|
| *Heat* magazine (1 per week) | £2,900 |
| Chocolate bar (1 per day) | £6,767 |
| Daily newspaper (Mon–Sat) | £7,733 |
| Mobile calls (per month) | £13,533 |
| Sky TV (£33 per month) | £19,333 |
| Starbucks coffee (1 per day) | £32,867 |
| Pint beer (1 per day) | £37,700 |
| Spurs season ticket | £46,400 |
| Cigarettes (20 per day) | £75,400 |
| 50 litres petrol (per week) | £90,867 |

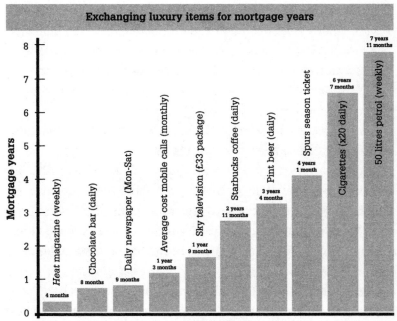

Exchanging luxury items for mortgage years

## CASE STUDIES

Simon and Debbie had such a luxurious lifestyle that they were almost spoilt for choice when it came to budgeting. Just cutting out monthly visits to the hairdresser and beautician would save £310, and not eating out would leave them £435 better off.

Julie, too, had lots of scope to rein in her spending. Did she really need that £650 coat? And surely she could cancel that order for a new Mercedes SLK?

Duncan could ill afford it, but he was always buying things that took his fancy. If only he could stop doing this for a while, he would soon be much better off. His daily treat of coffee at only £2 per day, every day of the year, adds up to an expenditure of over £700.

## Holidays

Many families will spend a fortune each year on family holidays. The Binners, for example, spend about £6,000. If you can't do without your annual break, why not consider taking camping holidays for a few years? Before you screw up your nose disdainfully and skip over this section, take a moment to consider the facts.

Camping is not necessarily the experience it once was. Modern, easy-to-erect dome tents in space-age designs create very comfortable living spaces. No longer is it a case of shivering beneath leaky canvas in a muddy field, or heating yet more beans on a rickety stove: most campers these days prefer bar meals. Up-to-date campsites have terrific amenities: modern shower blocks, kitchen and washing facilities and, in many cases, shops, entertainment and even pubs on site.

Camping with small children is especially rewarding. They enjoy the adventure and the fact that their playground begins just outside the door (well, tent flap), and with all that fresh air, they sleep well too.

Still think camping's too infra dig? A recent survey by Mintel revealed that it is mainly the AB socio-economic group (doctors, lawyers and other professionals) that is heading up the big camping holiday revival. Destinations on the north Cornwall coast are particularly popular; Polzeath, for example, has a large, clean beach and ready access to surfing lessons. Before you know it, you'll be like Dan and Lucy – getting up early to check out the surf and catch some waves. And as Dan points out, 'the sea is free.'

Spend an evening browsing the 'Great Outdoors' and 'Where I live' pages of the BBC website (see page 186) for some good places to visit. Sean and Anne-Marie waited until the last minute and booked a four-day break at a Haven holiday park in Weymouth. They stayed in a mobile home and went to their nearest supermarket to stock up on food. The holiday expenses were reduced further because all entertainment on site was free. Arthur and Mary also managed to go on a cheap holiday; they drove to La Rochelle in France with friends (sharing a car to cut down on petrol costs) then stayed with them rent-free in return for helping out with DIY on their French property.

## Food

Grocery shopping is another area where large savings are possible without compromising on what you eat. With a bit of forward planning, the grocery bill can be sliced and diced to cook up yet more savings to put towards paying off the mortgage. Lucy, for example, collected nettles from local hedgerows to produce fantastic soup – a meal that benefited the family's health as well as their finances. Mary and Arthur began to shop much more carefully, and tried out new ingredients to ring the changes. Quinoa wasn't a great success, but they loved lentils.

---

**TOP TIP**

**If foraging or looking for food in the wild, make sure you properly identify safe foodstuffs. Richard Mabey's book *Food for Free* (Collins) can keep you on the right track.**

---

Write down a list of meals that you enjoy and that are easy to prepare – you'll be surprised how long a list you can come up with. Then cross out any meals you buy ready-prepared (generally far more expensive than the sum of the ingredients they contain) and vow not to buy them any more. In order to save some money you will need to get cooking and invest a little time, but it needn't be hard work – and you might even enjoy it.

The food section of the BBC website is a comprehensive and easy-to-use source, containing some wonderful meal ideas. It can guide you through making toast and boiling an egg to more complex recipes, such as chocolate and orange soufflé.

When you have your list of meals, concentrate on those that can be made with less expensive ingredients, and plan your menus for the next fortnight. Cottage pie, spaghetti bolognese, sausage and mash – the possibilities for reasonably priced meals are limitless.

Make a shopping trip to pick up as many ingredients as you can in advance. Don't be tempted to waiver from your list and add more expensive items to your basket. If you have children, it is a good idea to leave them with a sitter while you are out shopping. It's amazing how much influence they can have during a shopping trip – a fact not lost on the supermarkets, who position tempting treats accordingly.

It is also important not to go food shopping when you are hungry because you'll simply be tempted to buy more than you need.

It is those shopping trips you make on the way home to 'pick up something for dinner' that tend to be the most expensive. Try to limit your purchases to fresh fruit and vegetables that you know you will use, and try buying a few more own-brand products (which are often manufactured by the named brands anyway), especially when you are combining items in a recipe. You don't have to commit to buying these items for the rest of your life, just give them a try. If you spot mega bargains like 'two for one', it can be worth bulk buying – as long as you use them before the use-by date, or can freeze them.

## Travel

How many times have you jumped into the car to make a short trip down the road, even when the weather was good or the journey would have been quicker on foot? We've all done it, and have wasted a lot of money in the process.

<u>**CASE STUDIES**</u>

Arthur and Mary decided to sell their second car, and Mary began to cycle everywhere, which was as good for her health as her pocket. Dan, on the other hand, sold his beloved motorbike and took to a more unusual form of transport. Every morning, he would hop on his skateboard and speed off to work, often racing alongside his sons as they skateboarded their way to school.

Where possible consider walking, cycling or using public transport. You will be saving money, getting fitter and saving the environment.

*Walking*

Getting about on foot can be fun, costs nothing and is suited to any lifestyle or circumstances. It also offers many health benefits:

- Lower blood pressure
- Reduced body fat
- Better flexibility and coordination
- Reduced risk of coronary disease and stroke
- Stronger bones

## 'Walking is the nearest activity to perfect exercise.'
Prof. Adrianne Hardman, sports scientist, Loughborough University

For fitness, 'brisk' walking is recommended. (This means walking at a pace where you should be able to hold a conversation without getting out of breath. Any faster and you may be jogging.) Committed dieters will know that walking 1.6 km (1 mile or about ten minutes) will burn up at least 100 calories – the equivalent of 1½ apples, a chocolate digestive or half a pint of beer.

You might think that walking into town instead of taking the car will not save much money, but add up the cost of petrol and parking over time, and you'll see that it can make a significant contribution to your budget (as well as your waistline). Mandy MacVean has benefited from leaving the car at home and walking to work instead.

Walking is good for the whole family. In 1999 the Health Education Authority estimated that children walk more than 80 km (50 miles) a year less than they did just ten years ago, and only half of Britain's 11–16-year-olds walk for ten minutes a day. Instead of ferrying your children around or allowing them to spend most of their free time in front of the television or computer, encourage them to get moving under their own steam. You can start your 2012 Olympic gold medal hopefuls on the right track today.

When out walking together as a family, not only will you notice much more than you do when speeding past in the car, but small children will view it as an adventure, especially if the walk is combined with something interesting, such as feeding the ducks in the park, visiting the playground or rambling through woods. The benefits of walking will amount to much more than pounds in your pocket.

*Cycling*

If walking isn't feasible or doesn't appeal, why not invest in a bicycle (or just dust down the one in the garage) and hit the national cycle network? This spans 16,000 km (10,000 miles) and includes some of the safest and most attractive routes in the UK – which perhaps explains why 40% of bicycle journeys are made for recreational purposes.

The network links up schools, town centres and railway stations and is well signposted, and up to one-third is traffic freeas it goes along disused railway lines, canal towpaths, riversides and parks;

the remainder is on quiet roads and in traffic-calmed areas. As almost 75% of the UK population lives within 3 km (2 miles) of the cycle network, it's a great way to get around. A great website which tells you all you need to know is www.sustrans.co.uk (see page 187).

## DID YOU KNOW?

**In the UK 2% of journeys are made by bicycle, compared to 10% in Germany. Statistics suggest that the Dutch and Germans are five times more likely to cycle to work than the British.**

## CASE STUDIES

Apart from using her bicycle to go out foraging for food, Lucy used it to get to her yoga classes. This saved money on petrol and she also found it very invigorating. Julie is saving the pennies by walking to work rather than catching the bus.

When you are buying a bicycle it pays to remember where you will be using it. Some mountain bikes include advanced suspension, thick tyres and no mudguards, so are not particularly useful if you will be cycling mainly on roads and cycle paths. Try not to be seduced by the marketing image. As with many other things in life, you get what you pay for and it is generally advisable to avoid very cheap bicycles. Around £200 should buy a suitable machine. Assuming you will not be riding up and down mountains regularly, look out for the following features:

- Comfortable saddle
- Mudguards
- Gears that are easy to operate
- Correct frame size for your height – get the salesperson
  to help you
- Chain protector

Keep an eye on advertisements in the local paper, as good bikes can often be picked up second-hand at a fraction of their original cost. Most cycle shops these days will service a used bike for a small charge.

Remember that while the initial outlay on a bike and accessories may seem expensive, you'll soon recoup what you would have paid in fares. The cost of a zone 1 and 2 travel card in London, for example, will be saved in just ten weeks.

## Petrol

Given the current high price of petrol, it is easy to see how walking, cycling and taking the bus will save you money. If, at a conservative estimate, you fill your car with petrol every two weeks, you will use more than £1,000 worth each year. Even a modest cut in car use can result in a saving that can be set aside to repay the mortgage. Remember, an extra £110 per month off a £150,000 mortgage saves nearly £32,000.

During 2004 and 2005, the price of crude oil shot up and those increases were reflected at the petrol pump and on the fuel surcharge levied by airlines. The price of oil seems to be driven as much by political events in the Middle East as by increased demand from countries such as India and China, where manufacturing output has increased. While the oil price rise has not had the same dramatic impact on inflation as similar price rises during the 1970s, there is a concern that this will begin to happen and many commentators predict further rises still. All in all, it seems that there has never been a better time to ditch the car for the benefit of both our wallets and our health.

If you have two or more cars, consider the possibility of getting by with just one. If you take one to work and it spends all day in a car park, could you use public transport instead? Being driven to work in a bus or train is less stressful than driving and frees up time to read the paper or a book, or even to get stuck into work a little bit sooner, earn more money and pay off your mortgage earlier.

While it's clear that considerable savings can be made in petrol, tot up all the other costs associated with running a vehicle, such as insurance, tax, servicing, parking and any hire purchase agreement. Getting rid of those expenses can bring paying off your mortgage that much closer. If the car is owned and not financed, so much the better: the sale proceeds can immediately be offset against the mortgage.

### CASE STUDY

The Holleymans have reduced costs by replacing their car with another, more economical, one and they are keeping their use of it to a minimum.

## Coffee

A daily cappuccino on the way to work may not seem like an extravagance, but when you consider that it costs £500 per year (250 coffees at £2 each), it is easy to see where an extra £50 or £100 per month can be found for the mortgage. Why not take a piece of fruit to work instead, or pester the boss to buy a cappuccino machine for the office? Duncan has made a real effort to cut back on the amount of expensive coffees he drinks every week.

## Cigarettes

A look around your local bookshop will show you that there are loads of books written on the subject of giving up smoking. The health benefits of quitting are undeniable, but let's take a quick look at the financial consequences of stopping smoking.

Cigarettes cost about £5.20 a packet, and the average smoker will spend more than £2,000 a year on them. Simply cutting your cigarette intake by half will therefore have an extraordinary effect on how quickly you can repay your mortgage.

A 20-a-day smoker for 20 years will set fire to the equivalent of:

• Two sports cars
• 63 mediterranean holidays
• 152 weekends at a health spa
• Six years' worth of mortgage repayments

Stopping smoking can also mean cheaper life and health cover once you've satisfied your insurer that you've really given up – for ever.

For more information on the best way to kick the nicotine habit contact the NHS smoking helpline (see page 187) and don't give up on giving up.

### René says

## Saving is important but controlling expenditure is vital

Self-discipline is important. Savings alone will not pay off your mortgage. Budget your expenditure and stick to it. However, leave yourself enough for a few treats when you hit significant milestones – you have to feel good about yourself and relate to those around you, and bread and water alone will not make you sparkling company!

## Eating out and socializing

An old joke claims that 'you don't live longer if you give up ciga-rettes and drink ... it just seems longer'. For many of us socializing represents a large proportion of our budget, and it can be very diffi-cult to compromise. If, however, you are serious about repaying your mortgage early, you should look for savings wherever possible. It would be foolish to dine high on the hog at expensive restaurants every week, or drink only champagne when you do go out. Cutting back is very different from cutting out, so remember this when you're trying to economize.

### CASE STUDIES

For some people, such as the MacVeans, eating out is an occasional treat to mark a birthday or anniversary. For oth-ers, such as the Binners, it's a way of life – and in their case they spend £500 a month on it. When it reaches this level, it's an obvious area in which to economize, and a relatively painless way to make savings.

Duncan, on the other hand, is a great cook and loves enter-taining, but this can be a great expense when done lavishly and often – as he does. Having fewer dinner parties and cooking simpler meals are obvious ways of economizing.

The Holleymans also love socializing and need little excuse to throw a party. This is something they've virtually given up in order to save money, but they've been so successful in their budgeting that they can still afford to indulge themselves occasionally.

## The good life

Of course, budgeting can be taken to extremes. In *The Good Life* (1975), when Richard Briers and Felicity Kendal abandoned the rat race for self-sufficiency in suburbia, it seemed to strike a chord with the nation. Escaping the office treadmill and living off the land will remain a dream for many, and may be a better premise for a sitcom than a plan for life, but growing your own produce can be a valuable money-saving strategy.

Don't have a garden or enough space to grow your own? What about renting an allotment from your local council? It doesn't cost a lot, and the National Association of Allotment and Leisure Gardeners website (see page 187) provides useful information on getting started which can equally be applied to your garden vegetable patch. The MacVeans decided to get an allotment and to grow their own veg – they think that as a result they have saved approximately £20 per week on their shopping bill.

## SIMPLE STEPS TO SAVE MONEY

### Make your own lunch

Sure, it's a pain in the neck having to make sandwiches and put together a packed lunch, but it takes only a few minutes each day and the cost savings are remarkable. You will find that you are preparing a week's lunches for what you once spent in a day or two at the sandwich shop. That £5 per day you'll be saving equals £1,300 saved over a working year. Why not try making a large batch of soup or stew at the weekend and take some to work in a flask for a cheap and nutritious lunch?

### Write down what you spend

This may seem a little strange – after all, you know what you spend your money on, don't you? Actually, keeping track of outgoings is a must when budgeting. Make a note of everything you spend, every single penny, and review it on a weekly basis to see where economies can be made. This may sound simple, but it is an incredibly powerful exercise and can lead to huge savings. It is also fascinating, and you will probably be astounded at where your money goes. The simple fact is that in the 21st century many of us are in the habit of spending money without realizing that we are doing it.

The Binners are a case in point. Their outgoings were an astonishing £5,314 a month. They knew they lived well, but were surprised at what they spent. By budgeting properly and keeping track of expenditure they have the potential to save as much as 50% of the cost of their mortgage.

## Pay off your credit card bill in full each month

According to the Financial Services Authority (*Risk Outlook 2005*), over a quarter of families have at least one credit card where the outstanding balance is not cleared each month. This was true of all our contributors, and they were wasting an amazing amount of money in the process. If you are doing the same, you could be wasting a fortune in interest. Spending money via a plastic card is psychologically easier than handing over £10 notes, but if you parted with real money, would you spend as much or as easily?

In May 2005 average consumer borrowing via credit cards, motor and retail finance deals, overdrafts and unsecured personal loans rose to an average of £4,071 for every adult – a 45% increase since 2000. Finance is not rocket science: if you can't afford to pay your bill at the end of the month, you shouldn't have spent the money. If you know you can't afford a purchase, save up for a month or two until you can. If you regularly can't pay off the bill, cut up your credit card(s) without hesitation. Budgeting takes discipline, and credit card borrowing is a false economy. If you have a balance that will take some time to pay off, move it to a card with a long interest-free period and a low APR and set about repaying it as soon as possible. Consumer websites, such as Moneyextra's (see page 187), provide comparisons of credit card charges.

## Open a savings account

It might sound stupid, but if you don't already have a savings account, open one right now and put aside 5% of your income. Don't try to save into your normal current account each month

– it's much too tempting to dip into it. The advantage of a savings account is that it's separate and you'll get a buzz from seeing the balance increase. Saving is contagious and has a wonderfully liberating effect: you really do sleep better at night with a few pounds in the bank.

Look for an account with a good rate of interest, but not necessarily one where the money is easily accessible. Perhaps open an account with a building society in a neighbouring town, or in two names so that two signatures are required for any withdrawal. That will make you pause for thought and keep a tighter rein on your spending.

## Get a second job

You may feel that you work hard enough, but if you are truly serious about paying off the mortgage early, a second job could be just the ticket to financial freedom. It might even be fun. If stacking shelves doesn't appeal, try to follow your interests and get a job in a bar, a football stadium, a wine shop or a cinema.

Depending on the nature of your second job, either you or your employer will have to pay any extra tax or National Insurance. The Holleymans took on extra work as office cleaners, earning £20 for a four-hour stint. Although this isn't a huge sum, their philosophy is that every little bit helps. Duncan, too, supplements his income by going round local pubs on Friday and Saturday nights giving Indian head massages. He asks the clients how much they think their massage was worth and gets approximately £5 per head.

## Cancel your gym membership

Do you actually use it? Even keep-fit fanatics can find other ways of staying in shape that won't cost a fortune. Try walking, jogging or cycling, or invest in a workout DVD. Anne- Marie and Duncan both found they saved considerable amounts of money by giving up their gym memberships.

## Make cards and gifts

It may seem mean to point this out, but the mark-up on greeting cards is extortionate. No wonder there are so many card shops around – it's big business. Count up the number of cards you send in a year – birthdays, Father's Day, Mother's Day, Valentine's Day, anniversaries, engagements, christenings, thank you's, moving house – the list goes on and on, and that's not including Christmas. What's your total? £50? £100? Go along to your local craft shop and you can buy the materials to make 20 cards for the cost of one.

Similarly, a gift you make can mean more to the recipient than one you buy because they know you have put your heart into it. For Dan and Lucy's son's ninth birthday, they each made him gifts. Dan made him a reading light from a VW Beetle headlight, and Lucy used an oddment of camouflage fabric to make him some wall-hung storage pockets. Both gifts cost just pennies, but their son was delighted.

## Play to your strengths

There is no **golden rule** or approach to follow, but it's better to **focus** on things you are really good at. For example, Duncan is a first class ballet dancer, he must capitalise upon this and so teaching fitness around ballet makes perfect sense. Speculating on the stock market, however, does not.

*'Money never starts an idea; it is the idea that starts the money.'*
Cameron, W. J., businessman

# Chapter 7
# Investing

**The stock market** is important to many of us as endowments are often largely based on returns from stocks and shares. Some people try to invest in the stock market to make money quickly in order to pay off their mortgage early. This is a risky strategy. The stock market can go down as well as up. Perhaps the best way of considering the stock market in the context of your mortgage is to invest there once you have paid off your mortgage, rather than trying to use it as a means of paying it off early.

## The stock market

When stock markets are going up, the lure of easy money can be intoxicating, and it is easy to understand why. Between 1995 and 1999 the UK economy was booming, as measured by the year-on-year increase in the value of the FTSE 100 share Index illustrated in the graph below.

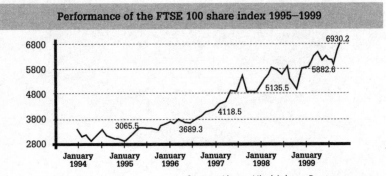

**Performance of the FTSE 100 share index 1995–1999**

Source: Lipper Hindsight, a Reuters company

The information shown in the performance graph opposite can be simplified as follows:

| Annual performance of the FTSE 100 share index, 1995–99 | |
| --- | --- |
| **Year** | **Performance** |
| 1995 | + 20.35% |
| 1996 | + 11.63% |
| 1997 | + 24.69% |
| 1998 | + 14.55% |
| 1999 | + 17.81% |

Source: Lipper Hindsight, a Reuters company

With an average return of over 15% each year, it is easy to see why many people were tempted to invest their spare cash in shares rather than immediately seek to repay their mortgage. An investment of £5,000 in FTSE 100 companies on 1 January 1995 would have grown to more than £13,000 by the end of the millennium when capital growth and company dividends were taken into account.

A similar lump sum investment in shares of £5,000 on 1 January 1995 followed by a monthly investment of £100 until 31 December 1999 would have given a return of more than £23,000. If the same amount had been set against a capital and interest mortgage with 15 years to run at an interest rate of 6%, the outstanding mortgage term would reduce from 15 years to 12 years and 10 months, saving just over £14,000 in repayments.

With hindsight, it is clear that investing in the UK stock market during this period was significantly more effective than making additional mortgage repayments. On the face of it, this is to be expected: simple mathematics tells us that we are better off investing in an asset that increases at an average rate of 15% each year than reducing a debt that is costing us just 6% per year.

Similar logic tells us that, given a choice, we should reduce short-term debts incurring high interest such as credit cards and store cards, rather than our mortgage, which is a lower cost, long-term debt.

## DID YOU KNOW?

**The London Stock Exchange can trace its history back more than 300 years, having begun in Jonathan's Coffee House in 17th-century London. When brokers erected their own building in 1773, it was briefly known as New Jonathan's, before members began calling it the Stock Exchange.**

The problem with investing in the stock market as a strategy for repaying the mortgage is that returns are not always as healthy as they were at the end of the 20th century. Consider the performance of the FTSE 100 over the subsequent five years to the end of 2004.

| Annual performance of the FTSE 100 index, 2000–04 | |
|---|---|
| Year | Performance |
| 2000 | - 10.21% |
| 2001 | - 16.15% |
| 2002 | - 24.48% |
| 2003 | + 13.62% |
| 2004 | + 7.54% |

Source: Lipper Hindsight, a Reuters company

Here we see that UK shares, in line with global stock markets in general, experienced a three-year bear market between 2000 and 2002, when prices fell, followed by a recovery. Over this five-year period the average return equated to an average loss of 6% (- 6%) each year. In this instance the strategy of reducing the mortgage would have been a clear winner, as a similar stock market investment of £5,000 on 1 January 2000, followed by a monthly investment of £100 until 31 December 2004, would have resulted in a return of just £10,400 – £600 less than the total amount invested.

So it all depends on timing and how the stock market performs. To be safe rather than sorry, it's best to pay off debt rather than speculate on the stock market.

## CASE STUDY

Uniquely among the participants in the series, Debbie and Simon had a substantial capital sum that they could invest to help pay off their mortgage in the future. I was concerned about this because once you move away from 'safe' savings, such as bank and building society accounts, into areas such as the stock market, you run the risk of losing money. This was particularly true as the initial experiment was to run for two years – not enough time to be confident that the returns from a stock market investment would be better than those from a bank or building society. Any adviser worth his salt wouldn't let them do it. Over five years, perhaps. Even then, you would want to be cautious.

Clearly, equity investments can play a part in paying off your mortgage early, but they are effective only when stock markets are rising. This begs the question: To what extent can market returns be predicted?

# Predicting investment returns

No matter what you hear to the contrary, it is impossible to predict the short-term direction that investment markets will take. Commentators who forecast performance tomorrow, next week or next month are, at best, making an educated guess. In the 21st century, economies have been driven as much by geopolitical events as they have by commercial and financial considerations. Looking at the longer-term picture, however, it should be possible to predict the future movement of asset classes (such as shares, property and fixed-interest investments) with a fair degree of accuracy.

Where, then, does this leave borrowers? Trying to time investments is extremely difficult, and if they are made at the wrong time, the capital value of the investments will fall. An alternative strategy is to remain in less volatile asset classes, such as cash or fixed-interest securities, but by following this approach you will be hard put to match the interest 'cost' of not using the funds to repay your mortgage. You'll also run the risk of missing out on any upward movement of the market, which can often happen quickly and dramatically.

There are two questions that should be asked. What are the long-term prospects for financial markets? Do present market levels represent good value? At the time of writing, the answers, as far as the UK stock market is concerned, are 'good' and 'yes'.

The following graph illustrates the likelihood of a positive return from investments over a number of time periods, based upon experience over the last 50 years in the USA, the world's largest stock market. What it tells us is that if you invest for one year, you have a 73% chance of achieving a positive return, which increases to 89% over five years and 93% over ten years. In no 20-year time frame, even including the Great Depression of the 1920s, has the US stock market failed to record positive growth.

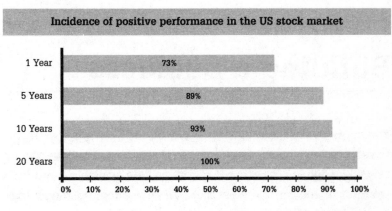

**Incidence of positive performance in the US stock market**

| | |
|---|---|
| 1 Year | 73% |
| 5 Years | 89% |
| 10 Years | 93% |
| 20 Years | 100% |

Source: Thomson Wealth Management

Of course, a 20-year time frame is not much use when you are planning to repay your mortgage early. In the UK the average one-year return for equity investments over the past 80 years is +9.12%, while the average five- and ten-year returns are equally impressive at +50.94% and +116% respectively. However, as the period 2000–04 demonstrated, past performance is no guarantee of future returns. As far as your mortgage is concerned, it is a question of certainty. The loan isn't going to melt away, so the best option is almost always to pay off your mortgage early rather than play the stock market.

*'The safest way to double your money is to fold it over and put it in your pocket.'*
Frank McKinney Hubbard, American writer and artist (1868-1930)

# Chapter 8
# Building a Business

**You know** by now that in order to pay off your mortgage early, you have to increase your repayments to the bank or building society, as well as budget. Fine, but what options are available if you don't want to sell the car or get another job? How about building a business of your own?

Take a look at the list below. Many of the people at the top branched out on their own with a business idea at some time or another – why not you and why not now?

*The Times* **Rich List 2004**
1. Roman Abramovich, £7,500m, Oil, football and investments
2. Duke of Westminster, £5,000m, Property
3. Hans Rausing and family, £4,950m, Food packaging
4. Philip Green, £3,610m, Retailing
5. Lakshmi Mittal, £3,500m, Steel
6. Sir Richard Branson, £2,600m, Transport and mobile phones
7. Kirsten and Jorn Rausing, £2,575m, Inheritance, bloodstock and investments
8. Bernie and Slavica Ecclestone, £2,323m, Motor racing
9. Charlene and Michel de Carvalho, £2,260m, Inheritance, brewing and banking
10. David and Simon Reuben, £2,200m, Property and metal trading

There are a few basic principles that are worth bearing in mind before racing off to look around factories, calling Manchester United to negotiate shirt sponsorship, or contacting the BBC to tell them that you want to replace Sir Alan Sugar in the next series of *The Apprentice*.

For starters, you will need a plan. A business is worth nothing unless it has an infrastructure that gives it the best chance of success. Until that point, a good idea is nothing more than an idea. A classic mistake made by people entering business for the first time is to believe that their idea is all they need – that they can sell their idea for millions, or that a large organization will provide them with the resources to manufacture their product. This may be what happens in films, but the reality is not as simple as that.

## CASE STUDY

Among the contributors to our experiment, only Heather and Chloe had drawn up a plan. It was inches thick and very detailed, for which they apologized, but I was impressed. It outlined everything they wanted to do in terms of their decluttering and childrens' party businesses and included growth projections and spin-off ideas, but there was one major omission: they had no numbers. This told me a lot about the way Heather and Chloe thought and planned – impressive up to a point, but lacking financial awareness.

## TOP TIP

**As difficult as it is, you must, must grind out the numbers. They can tell you a lot: whether your idea is realistic, the milestones you need to reach, and when you should reach them. If you can't work out the numbers yourself, get help from someone with the relevant experience.**

## René says

**You don't have to be great at business**

It is important to have budgets and plans in **proportion** to the task. It is not necessary to have a fully fledged business with profit and loss accounts. Keep it really simple and ensure you have the necessary **controls** in place.

## Drawing up a business plan

Setting down your thoughts in a business plan gives life to your idea, and adds flesh to the bones of your proposition and helps you to demonstrate how it might develop. A good business plan will outline how you envisage bringing your idea to market, testing the concept and determining the future of your business, while identifying the milestones ahead. It will help you to improve your company, persuade others to back your vision and, in time, become the basis on which you review the direction in which you are heading.

As well as painting in the broad brushstrokes, your business plan should demonstrate that you have thought through the details: dates, deadlines, fixed costs, raw materials, suppliers, competitor analysis, unit costs, manufacturing and process resources, your marketing and distribution strategy, management infrastructure and, most importantly, who is going to buy your idea and how you will look after them. Even if your business does not involve manufacturing something, most of these details will still apply.

Your business plan should sell both your idea and your strategy for turning it into profits. In fact, it's sensible to regard your plan as a blueprint for how you will run the business, not simply a necessary evil in order to get it up and running. Putting things in writing will clarify them for you as much as everyone else. Remember that banks and financial backers see hundreds of business plans, and can quickly tell if a plan is formulaic and cursory. For example, don't simply project year-on-year sales growth: explain how and where it will be generated. Potential backers are looking for much more than a good idea. They want you to demonstrate that you have the requisite communication, professional and managerial skills to make your business flourish.

## QUESTIONS YOUR BUSINESS PLAN SHOULD ANSWER

If the effort you've put into your plan appears superficial, potential backers will be unlikely to lend you money. At the very least your business plan should address the following questions.

- What is your product or service?
- What is your market?
- Who is your competition?
- How will you reach your customers?
- Who is involved?
- What are your financial expectations?
- How much money do you need?
- What are the risks?

In addition, your plan should include your thoughts on the following topics.

### Your goal

In this section you will need to detail the concept and how it took shape. Set out a vision for your business and where you expect it to be in six months, one year, three years and five years. Keep details to a minimum, but ensure that you can demonstrate milestone progressions for your company at each stage of the process. Investors will think you naive if you show your operation at critical mass three months after launch, with no competition and 100% market share. This is your opportunity to provide an overview of the business, and you should regard it as your one and only chance to make a pitch to potential investors. It should demonstrate your enthusiasm for the project and that you have the necessary acumen, knowledge and abilities to carry it off. You should detail that you have an understanding of what is required in terms of resources, both financial and physical, and that you are aware of the risks involved. You should inspire confidence that you understand the key drivers of your proposition and have the ability to execute your plan.

## TOP TIP

**Be realistic when building a plan. A good rule of thumb is to assume that seven out of ten things will go against you.**

## René says

## Collaborate

Nothing is best done alone any more, especially paying off your mortgage. Identify a partner to work with you on this. Everybody will need support, encouragement, a bit of a push and someone to celebrate the successes with.

## CASE STUDY

Dan's main business strategy is to manufacture high-value items, such as his stoves, because consumers will pay a premium for something that is unusual and handmade, and that has the additional attraction of an interesting heritage – namely, Dan's story.

His second strategy is to knock out lower-value items, such as candlesticks and fire tongs, as fast as he can (without compromising quality), and as cheaply as possible. He has a friend whom he could employ on a part-time basis to do this for him while he concentrates on the real money-making ideas. With both angles, Dan needs a lot of help to develop a distribution, sales and marketing strategy.

Dan reckons he can easily make two stoves a week. If he can sell just one a week for £1,000 over two years, he could make £100,000 income from them. Making them, however, should be the easy part. Finding distributors is going to be the secret to success. Any volume sales of candlesticks and so on is going to be a bonus. Again, distribution is going to be the key, but this time he will need to be shifting the items in volume. This means selling to retail outlets in Cornwall, and possibly mail order through associated car magazines (particularly to sell the old car camshafts that he has made into candlesticks) and the Internet.

## Your market

In order to survive and prosper, businesses require one thing – customers. In this section of your plan you must clearly define who they will be, provide specific examples and back these up with market research and analysis. Be as specific as possible about your buyers' motives for purchasing your product – what benefit (real or perceived) they will derive from it. Will they continue to purchase in the future, and why should they purchase from you? Detail the mistakes that your potential competitors are making and how you will avoid falling into the same traps. Support your conclusions with as much information, research and evidence as you can.

Provide specific details to demonstrate that you know your market. Name your potential customers, if you can, detail where they are and state what might influence their buying decisions. Outline your marketing and sales strategy and how you plan to distribute your product or service. Demonstrate an understanding of potential competitors and what drives their businesses. How are their products costed and marketed? Does the market rely upon bulk discounts, price differentials or special offers? If possible, anticipate how your competitors will react to your business.

Your plan should show that your business is sustainable. It may be difficult to obtain funding for a venture that can operate only by taking advantage of a single opportunity, especially one that is time limited such as fashion items like clothes, popular drinks or the 2012 Olympics.

## CASE STUDIES

Market restrictions were probably going to put paid to the ideas of at least three of our contributors. Heather and Chloe's plan to restart their decluttering business in Cornwall had two things against it: the first is that Cornwall is a relatively poor area with less disposable income than Edinburgh, so a rate of £40 per hour might just be too much; and the second is that the Cornish are less sophisticated than city types (I come from Cornwall, so I can say this).

In the past they had never needed to advertise because they received glowing word-of-mouth testimonials. One customer even reckoned that their efforts had increased the value of his house by £20,000 when he sold it. Perhaps they could look at expanding the decluttering business to include dressing houses for sale. They could use pictures of their delighted Scottish vendor's home as a testimonial. In order to hit the numbers they need now, they can't rely solely on word-of-mouth advertising as they have done in the past. They need to market themselves, but neither has any experience in this area. I feel that their best bet is to try to sell the concept of decluttering and/or dressing houses to other businesses, who could then introduce potential clients to them. For example, estate agents or – strange and morbid as it might sound – funeral directors, as well as solicitors and accountants: anyone whose line of work brings them into contact with property on a regular basis. This would need a careful approach with a fully thought-through strategy and sales process. Achievable, but not easy.

Being based in Cornwall will also inhibit Lucy's ambition to be the best yoga teacher in the world. The market for yoga classes in her corner of the country is limited by the number of people living there, and the money to be made is dictated by the amount they will be willing to pay. Lucy, in turn, is limited in the number of classes she can teach because there is only so much that one person can do. These realities put pressure on developing other commercial areas, such as DVDs, books and equipment. For these to sell, Lucy has to develop a personal brand and publicity around herself – probably on a national level. This is a tall order, particularly as she won't be keen on spending even short periods away from the family. The odds are therefore very much stacked against her fulfilling her ambition.

## TOP TIP

Accept that setbacks happen. Deal with them quickly and move on.

## Get help!

Never underestimate what **help and support** is available to you if you just ask. Your family and friends will have resources and contacts that you never dreamt of. Many opportunities for **generating income** are very close to you but might just need a fresh pair of eyes or hands to bring them to fruition.

Do not only use all the brains you have, but all **you can borrow**.

## You and your team

Provide details about the principal members of your business, even if it is just you and your partner, including CVs and biographies. Make sure you highlight any relevant experience and qualifications they have. If you anticipate appointing more staff in the future, detail the characteristics of the individuals that you would like to hire. Having the right people on board, or demonstrating that you know where to find them, will impress potential backers.

## Finances

Compile cash-flow forecasts and financial statements to cover all eventualities. Gain a working understanding of spreadsheets, or ensure that you have the support of someone who can help you to create them. Project two or three separate scenarios, perhaps anticipating higher than expected costs, fewer purchasers or potential delays, and demonstrate the effect that these will have on the business. Try to foresee any extra equipment or vehicles that you might need in the future and account for them in full. Investors are far more likely to buy into the concept if they feel that you have predicted and planned for all potential eventualities.

Begin by making a note of the known costs. Create a column for each month of the first three years and detail the (minimum) salary that you will take, as well as what you will pay any other members of staff, including your spouse. Remember to include inflationary salary increases for your staff, and to account for tax and National Insurance that you may have to pay as an employer. Include a summary column at the end of each year to detail the annual costs.

Next consider what other costs you expect to incur. What premises are required, in what location and at what price? How much will you pay for secretarial services, a computer, software, telephone, accountancy and legal services, as well as insurance and office sundries? With all of these, specify if they are one-off purchases, or to what extent you can forecast them as regular (and increasing) costs.

Include specific forecasts for income based upon unit sales, and balance this with the cost of production. What raw materials will you require and in what quantities? If the business requires a vehicle, detail the costs associated with it – tax, insurance, fuel, servicing, etc. Note the cost of any marketing material, printing costs and advertising, as well as the cost of any travelling you expect to do.

Above all, don't forget to include an allowance for loss somewhere in your figures. When detailing specific costs, entrepreneurs sometimes discover that their ideas are perhaps not as viable as they had first imagined.

Finally, detail what capital is required, when it is necessary and for what purpose you intend to use it. State what milestones will accompany the requirement for more funds, and detail how and when the business will begin to repay any borrowings. Investors will be eager to anticipate their exit strategy and profit, and far more likely to invest if they can understand when and how returns will be generated.

> ## TOP TIP
>
> **Having a financial target is critical. It focuses the attention on the activity required to meet it, rather than just trying something and trusting to luck, as many people do. If you are really serious about paying off your mortgage early, your target might be the amount of your mortgage after allowing for expenditure, tax and National Insurance.**

## CASE STUDY

When Heather and Chloe eventually worked them out, the numbers for their decluttering business seemed rather thin. Let's assume that they need to make £40,000 per annum and that they can charge £40 per hour.

£40,000 ÷ £40 per hour = 1,000 chargeable hours per annum
Let's assume 50 weeks a year:
1,000 hours ÷ 50 weeks = 20 hours a week
20 hours ÷ 5 days a week = 4 hours per day

These figures are probably unachievable from a standing start, but they are nonetheless illuminating. Only if Chloe works for four chargeable hours a day, five days a week, 50 weeks a year will they get to £40,000. On top of this, they have to come up with a successful sales and marketing plan, find target prospects and build in scalability – all while Heather's working full time. If they make £20,000 a year from this, they will be doing well. Still, £40,000 knocks a big hole in a £90,000 mortgage, and it's worth aiming high.

## TAKE THE INITIATIVE

Ask your local council about their business development initiatives. Organizations such as Business Link (see page 186), a support, advice and information service provided by the Department of Trade and Industry, can assist with example business plans, point out common pitfalls and mistakes, and advise you on the various schemes, resources and grants available for entrepreneurs.

Other organizations, such as registered accountants, run evening classes where experts are invited to lecture on topics relevant to business, which can be invaluable in helping you develop your ideas while in the planning stage. Our contributors Heather and Chloe were great at tapping into the intellectual capital and funding available at a local level.

### René says

## Know all your assets

Take the time to list all your assets, then work out what they are worth and which you are prepared to sell. Then, pause! Think clearly about what you would use the money for. It is best used to fund a money-making venture, so think carefully about when to sell.

*'The only place you find success before work is in the dictionary.'*
Vince Lombardi, football coach

## Other considerations

If applicable, anticipate what product or service developments may be required in the future. Also include an appendix of supporting materials, such as outline costs for any equipment and sample supplier agreements. Don't forget to report detailed market research responses, including any particularly helpful comments and observations that have been made, or how you have incorporated responses into the plans for your business.

## TOP TIP

**Make sure you really understand why you want to do something. This is essential if you are to keep motivated.**

## CASE STUDY

Mary Holleyman planned to use her connections in Egypt to purchase aromatherapy oils and perhaps jewellery, and import them (along with all the proper permissions, of course) to the UK, where she could sell them to:

- Clients
- Retail outlets
- Other aromatherapists
- Companies for whom she provided stress management services
- Individual shoppers on the Candy Crystal website

All at a whopping 600% margin.

Her plan would have to make clear that she recognized the need for buying in further skills, such as marketing, sales and distribution, to fully capitalize on these areas.

# Common pitfalls

There are a number of mistakes that commonly occur in the preparation of business plans.

✗ Too many plans are formulaic and reveal poor preparation. Remember that you are not filling in a questionnaire – you are creating something unique that is an opportunity to sell your business.

✗ Avoid overpraising your business, overestimating the size of the potential market or underestimating the strength of competitors.

✗ Don't give market data full of estimates and hypotheses, and unsupported by evidence.

✗ Never assume that the benefits to customers are apparent and that they will flock to purchase your product or service.

✗ Don't overegg the pudding. Present detailed information simply and succinctly, with a minimum of spreadsheets. Condense your findings in an executive summary, and include details in an appendix at the end of your plan.

## CASE STUDY

Debbie Binner's business plan seemed unfeasible even without being committed to paper. She wants to give up her day job and launch her own PR company. If she starts small, with one day a week of consultancy work at £500 per day for 50 weeks of the year, she can bring in £25,000, but this won't be easy from a standing start. She must outline where she will get her clients from and how she sees her client list growing.

During the time she is setting up and promoting her PR business, she also wants to be training as a yoga or Pilates instructor, so she must show how this slots into the equation. If she eventually manages four lessons per week at

£25 per lesson for 50 weeks, she will be looking at only £5,000 coming in over the two-year period, which is not a huge return and will impinge on the amount of time she can dedicate to her PR activities. These figures don't look good and the two ideas don't really mesh together.

Finally, a word of advice for anyone planning to escape from employeedom and who feels their frustration boiling over. No matter how satisfying the idea may be, it is never, never a good idea to march into your boss's office and tell him or her exactly what they can do with your job. Indeed, it would be particularly foolhardy if you are not already well advanced with your plans to start your own business and have not secured the required funding.

Hotheadedness and business are never good bedfellows. It can take several months of establishing a business before you can even begin to form relationships with potential customers, and a predictable cash flow may be a long way off. If you are taking the plunge, progress as far as you can in your spare time before leaving work and giving up your source of income and benefits.

## TOP TIP

Be aware of issues that may need specialist legal or technical advice when setting up a business. These could include child protection, health and safety, and data protection.

*'Drive thy business, let it not drive thee'*
Benjamin Franklin, American statesman and scientist (1706-90)

# The law

When you start out in business you will have to deal with a mind-boggling number of considerations and issues. A good piece of advice is to ensure that you get the legal ones right, as they are likely to be the most important. For a start, you will need to obtain advice on the legal structure of your venture: will you be a sole trader, go into partnership, or form a private limited company?

These are important considerations, so you should seek the advice of a suitably qualified and experienced solicitor. Ask friends or relatives if they have used a good solicitor. Personal experience is often better than a cold start with someone you know very little about. The legal structure of your venture will determine the finance laws that dictate your accounting practices, the records that you will be required to keep, and the way in which your business is structured. It will also determine the potential liability that you have if the business does not go according to plan.

For example, limited companies require Articles of Association – a statutory legal document that sets out in writing the way in which the company will be governed, the rights of the shareholders and the powers of the company directors. Limited companies must also have officers – directors and a company secretary – who must be part of your corporate structure at all times.

The following section details some of the legal factors that should be taken into account, but it is by no means a definitive list.

## Health and safety

Your working environment will be required to meet certain legal standards for health and safety. You must display the correct notices to staff and communicate your company policies to them. If your processes involve the use of harmful substances, dust, fumes or excessive noise, you are legally obliged to protect employees. Special rules apply where the operation of equipment and machinery is involved, or when staff are expected to work at heights or in confined spaces. The onus is on the employer to find out about his or her obligations.

Employees are protected by laws which, among other things, control the number of hours they can work, the rest breaks they can take and what they can be expected to lift and carry. When young people, generally under 18, are involved in the business, the rules are stricter still. They also dictate what is required on site in terms of first aid skills and equipment.

As an employer you will have to take out some compulsory insurance policies for things such as employer's liability. If you have five or more employees, there is even a legal requirement to arrange access for them to a pension scheme.

## Property

If you are not working from home, obtaining a site for your business will bring you into contact with the law. The right premises can make or break a business, and location is especially important for retail outlets such as shops and restaurants.

In arranging property, the legal considerations will include:

- Dealing with the property purchase or rental agreement, including negotiating the lease, rent reviews and rent-free periods
- Security and risk assessment
- Your responsibilities as a tenant, if applicable
- Disabled access and facilities
- Planning permission and building regulations

## Tax and accounting

The rules that dictate your responsibilities in this area are determined by the legal structure of your company, and will include:

- VAT registration

- Income tax and National Insurance (for employees and the self-employed)
- Corporation tax
- Companies House registration
- Stamp duty
- Environmental considerations and tax breaks
- Business expenses
- Vehicles, including company cars
- Benefits in kind, e.g. Mary Holleyman's aromatherapy and massages paid for by TNT
- Business rates payable to the local council

### CASE STUDY

Inadvertently, Mary fell foul of the tax office in her original aromatherapy and massage arrangement with TNT. Her massages were deemed to be taxable benefits in kind, which meant that the employees who received them would have to be taxed on them. By reshaping her business as stress management and offering a wider range of services, she hoped to overcome this problem and make the enterprise work again.

I could fill another book with details of the administrative and record-keeping responsibilities that being in business necessitates. Suffice it to say that it is important to retain the services of an accountant or bookkeeper and to keep meticulous records. Your business will need a bookkeeping system and profit and loss account, although specialist software is available that should make this job easier. If all else fails, make sure you keep your receipts in a safe place and employ somebody to update your books regularly. Failure to do so will hit you directly in the pocket, as you will end up paying more in tax.

Specific rules dictate the filing of tax returns, and it is important to follow these carefully. If not, you will face penalties for late filing and late payment of taxes, and, even worse, enquiries and tax inspections.

If your business is very successful, you may find that you eventually need to explore the legal consequences of selling it or of buying another. Alternatively, if things fail to go according to plan, there are further rules and regulations to observe in closing your business and handling insolvency and bankruptcy.

## Sales and marketing

Sales are the lifeblood of any business. To create an effective sales and marketing strategy you have to know who your customers are and what they need. After all, the purpose of your business will be to satisfy their requirements better than your competitors. Apart from being the key to building a successful business, sales are also the key to paying off your mortgage in double-quick time.

Marketing is the process of reaching new customers and keeping existing customers satisfied. It is in a permanent state of flux, so you will need to keep your strategy under constant review to ensure that you are maximizing the opportunities to stay ahead of the competition.

Try not to make the mistake of assuming that sales will simply happen. Just because you believe in your business, it doesn't mean that your potential customers will. Relying on word of mouth is also a classic mistake for small businesses. It is much better to start shouting from the roof tops yourself as soon as possible.

## CASE STUDY

Sean Casey-Poole wants to give up his day job and make a career of stage hypnotism. If he does only three shows a week for 40 weeks a year, and one job a week in neurolinguistic programming for the corporate market, he could make a huge dent in his mortgage, but it would put pressure on his marketing and distribution skills to get the required bookings in the first place. This is where Anne-Marie comes in. She works in marketing, so perhaps she can help get him the bookings by drawing up a proper marketing plan. All Sean would have to do is turn up and perform – which is what he loves doing anyway.

## A good starting point

Want to know what you're doing right – and wrong? What you need is a SWOT analysis (SWOT stands for Strengths, Weaknesses, Opportunities and Threats). This approach has been used by businesses for many years and has become something of a cliché, but it survives because it is so effective.

Start by writing down the four headings on a blank sheet of paper and make a note of anything in your business or business plan that falls under these categories. The following points might be useful in helping you to complete your SWOT analysis.

**Strengths**
- What do you do well?
- Specialist knowledge
- Unique product features

**Weaknesses**
- What do you do badly?
- Lack of capital
- Lack of after-sales service
- Lack of brand awareness

**Opportunities**
- The Internet
- New product developments
- Local events
- National and local demographic changes
- New property developments bringing new customers

**Threats**
- Competitors
- A slump in the market
- Changes in legislation
- Bad debts
- Poor assumptions

Try to take an objective look at your business, perhaps from the viewpoint of your customers. Better still, if you have an established operation, why not take a moment to speak to customers and ask their opinion? They will feel valued if you let them know that you respect their views, and be more likely to remain loyal to your business.

None of our contributors had done a SWOT analysis, but without exception they all needed to. Let's look at one poorly conceived idea.

## CASE STUDY

Anne-Marie planned to start holding weight-loss classes, and reckoned on getting 35 people to attend each one. I think this was far too optimistic from a standing start. She reckoned on holding 12 classes a week with each person paying £4.20 per class. At this point, I thought she must have taken leave of her senses: that's two classes a day for six days a week on top of a full-time job. The numbers looked fantastic. Perhaps a better word to describe them would be 'fantasy'. Maybe Sean had hypnotized her while I had been away. Given her family obligations and job, I felt that around £5,000 p.a., rather than the £26,000 p.a. she was planning, would be a great result. See what I mean about idealism? In business it only ever gets you so far.

## 'A business has to be involving, it has to be fun, and it has to exercise your creative instincts'
Richard Branson, British entrepreneur

### Beef up your tactics

Spend some time developing a marketing plan to concentrate your efforts where they will be most effective. A good strategy will take into account the needs of the customer and how these can best be met. This will help you to focus your energies on those customers who will be most profitable for you. Are there groups of customers who are particularly inclined towards your products or services? Where can you target them? Do they belong to a particular socio-economic group, or is your business targeted at individuals with a particular hobby or requirement?

What is the best method of communicating with your customers? Be careful to weigh up whether an email marketing campaign will interest or annoy them. The Internet has created multi-millionaire business people and has revolutionized the way in which many of us shop. How effective should the Web presence be for your business, and how much should you invest in it? Should you create an online shop, and what methods of payment should you accept?

Where possible, build in details of events, dates and any foreseeable costs, such as advertising or printing. If you are providing a product or service to another business, why not see if you can showcase what you do at a trade fair or with a professional organization? Try to maximize relationships with local and national media. An appearance in the papers or on the news could be very beneficial.

Set measurable targets by a specified deadline for any campaign and analyse the results to see if they have been effective, especially where there has been a capital outlay in, say, advertising or by providing a discount. Set aside time to do the analysis and assess whether your approach has been profitable. If the results are not what you want, be prepared to change your tactics.

In sales and marketing you sometimes have to take a long-term view with customers, but don't be tempted into offering your product or services at a loss to secure a new contract unless you have an established business.

Try to accentuate the benefits that your product or service will give to your customer rather than focusing on particular features. Make it exciting. In marketing speak, 'Don't sell the sausage, sell the sizzle'. Try to anticipate any objections that your customers may have and nullify them at the outset: 'You might think this widget is expensive, but think how much it will save you in the long term ...'

When creating a brand, make sure that it is one your customers can identify with. If you are targeting young, Internet-orientated companies, it will pay to have a dynamic image, but above all make sure it is professional. People prefer to do business with individuals who are like-minded. You needn't spend thousands on a logo: why not sponsor a competition at a local art school, provide a detailed brief and offer a £100 first prize for the best brand design?

Finally, don't take your customers for granted. Never assume that you know what they require, and always ensure that you make time for existing customers. Target them with a post-sales customer service questionnaire and remind them that they are important to you. Consider producing a newsletter or magazine to help generate repeat sales, especially if you are introducing new products or services.

## Working from home

It sounds fantastic, doesn't it? You are planning a new venture where there will be no commuting. You will have the freedom to begin work when you want, pop to the kitchen and make a sandwich when you need to, and have your favourite radio station playing in the background all day.

Think again. There is a definite skill to working from home, and it is not easy to master. Being aware of the pitfalls will make it easier to adjust to working in the spare bedroom.

The information given so far may seem rather daunting, but it is not intended to put you off – merely to give you the best possible opportunity to succeed. Remember the business maxim: 'If you fail to prepare, you prepare to fail.' As with all clichés, it contains an element of truth.

### 'The harder I work, the luckier I get'
Samuel Goldwyn, American film producer (1882-1974)

## TIPS FOR WORKING FROM HOME

- Create an obvious working environment for yourself at home. It is very easy to get distracted when you are surrounded by domestic paraphernalia.
- Ignore household chores until your working day is finished. When faced with a dull task, it is easy to give in to the temptation to mow the lawn, do the washing up or even take a nap on the basis that you would only have had to do it later.
- Keep strict working hours and treat them as seriously as you would in an office.
- Arrange to work in another environment now and then – working from home can be a lonely experience. A few days working at home and you soon appreciate the benefits of an office, and vice versa.
- Be professional and ignore the temptation to work in your pyjamas. Start the day by showering and getting dressed – exactly as if going into an office.
- Sort out child care if you have a young family. It may be tempting to imagine you can multitask, but toddlers demand a lot of attention and there is rarely space for anything else.
- Keep in touch. While being at home is fantastic for concentration, you will soon come to appreciate how useful it is to bounce ideas off colleagues. Create a new network so that you do not become cut off.
- Try to carve out an office at home as opposed to working at the dining-room table. A permanent workspace should have a door so that you can keep the world out – especially when you are on the telephone.
- Install a separate telephone line and Internet connection for business purposes. It should stop you getting embroiled in home life and means that you mark at the end of your working day by switching on the answer machine and closing the door.

## DID YOU KNOW?

American entrepreneurs Larry Page and Sergey Brin launched the Google search engine in 1998 from a friend's garage. With over 200 million 'hits' per day, Google is now comfortably the world's most popular search engine and was floated on the stock market in 2004 for more than $35 billion.

## Franchises

If building a business from scratch sounds daunting, why not consider opening a franchise? Franchise businesses grow not by traditional means of expansion, but by licensing others to sell an established brand or service.

As an investor in a business format franchise, you (the franchisee) will receive an information package of everything required to operate a business under an established brand and manage it with continued assistance from the franchisor. In return, you pay the franchisor a set-up fee, as well as ongoing charges, usually as a percentage of turnover or profits. For their part, the franchisor provides continued support, which will vary according to the franchise, but will usually include product development, training and advertising.

Franchises remove some of the risk in starting up in business as they are already proven concepts with demonstrable performance in other locations. Large, well-established franchises, such as McDonald's, Bang & Olufsen and Thorntons, offer customers a known brand and provide in-depth support to franchisees.

There are over 700 franchised businesses to choose from, and they generally fare very well in relation to other start-ups, with 96% of franchise units still operating profitably after five years. For more information contact the British Franchise Association (see page 186).

## What's to stop you succeeding?

There are numerous factors that could get in the way of your becoming the next Bill Gates. Perhaps most common is lack of time, particularly if you are working and have a family. Or perhaps you lack experience or knowledge and are unsure where to turn. Another common problem is lack of money, especially if you have diverted every spare penny towards paying off the mortgage. None of these issues is insurmountable, and it is worth pursuing your vision even if only to clarify that turning it into a viable business is not a practical proposition. Enterprise agencies are invaluable in steering you through the maze of red tape and identifying support schemes, such as the Prince's Trust (see page 187), which can assist entrepreneurs under the age of 30.

Of course, there may be other reasons that hold you back – perhaps a fear of the unknown, or a lack of support and enthusiasm from your spouse or family. These are much more difficult to overcome than resource problems, so you should think carefully and discuss your plans at length before making a decision.

Nobody is saying that paying off your mortgage early will be easy. In fact, it will be hard work and must involve sacrifices. The only certainty is that paying off your mortgage is much trickier if you work for somebody else. By starting your own business your earnings are potentially limitless. A quick flick through the biography of any successful businessperson will highlight two traits they have in abundance – determination and energy.

*'It's all about the quality of life and finding a happy balance between work and friends and family.'*
Philip Green, British businessman (1952–)

## Never, ever give up

**Many of the contributors have had to learn the hard way – by their mistakes. However, they have learnt and managed to move forward. See mistakes as necessary learning. Just don't make the same mistake twice. Life is not about how fast you run or how high you climb, but how high you bounce!**

*René says*

## Afterword

This experiment is about trying to pay off your mortgage early – it's not pretending to provide a thorough and comprehensive guide to setting up and running a business in every detail.

Naturally, once you have decided to start up a business you will need tax, legal and financial advice that is specific and appropriate to your own personal circumstances and your proposed business.

As well as the formal and financial issues, it is very important that you properly assess and fully understand all the issues that involve the amount of time, effort and energy you will need to devote to your new venture.

As someone famously once said, genius is 1% inspiration, 99% perspiration.

# Where Are They Now?

### Simon and Debbie Binner

Simon and Debbie probably face the hardest challenge of all the contributors to the series, in that they have the largest mortgage at £233,000. They are a successful and driven couple, however their greatest obstacle is their attachment to their luxury lifestyle. Over the course of the year, the couple were given a budget of £1,500 per month, which would give them a substantial saving on their usual outgoings of £5,314.

Debbie left her job and set up her own media-training company – which is going very well so far. Nothing came of Simon's teaching idea, but he has stuck to his guns and is concentrating on boosting his income and contribution to paying off the mortgage by trying to earn more commission on top of his high salary.

Their success in the second year of the experiment could be made more likely if they were to cut back on their lavish lifestye. As it is, success is made difficult by their inability to stick to their budgets and also by the time needed for their business ideas to start to work for them. Their commitment to putting all their efforts into making money also means they are feeling the strain of being part of the experiment and it is uncertain whether or not they will continue to be part of the series.

### Sean and Anne-Marie Casey-Poole

This family came on board determined to create some financial stability in their lives, believing that paying off their £85,000 mortgage would be a big step in this direction. They were set a budget of £155 per week – a budget they have tried to stick to, despite overspending by £85 a week in the first four months of the experiment.

Sean was keen to quit his job at the bank – and although he did so, after a rethink he returned to it part-time. He is now putting his efforts into neuro-linguistic programming for corporate clients. In addition to this work, he also plans to find a new agent in a bid to secure more shows for his comedy hypnotism act.

So, having laid the foundations for their new careers, only time and hard work will tell if they can make these ideas work over the next and final year in order to realize their dream and pay off their mortgage.

### Julie Edosa

With her children grown up, and a new partner in her life, Julie was

keen to pay off her £75,000 mortgage and free herself of a major financial burden. She began the experiment with great enthusiasm and lots of
ideas, but she too is hampered by an extravagant lifestyle. Initially, economizing went well but unfortunately, this was not to last.

Likewise, despite her initial flurry of ideas – including property spec-
ulation, selling cosmetics on the Internet, a weekly market stall and
letting out rooms in her house – her refusal to compromise her full-time
job to follow them up was limiting her chances of making real progress.
However, 2006 is looking better – she is moving out of her house to let it
to professionals and renting a room elsewhere in Bristol. The income left
over once she has paid for her room will go towards paying off her mortgage. Her business plan is now to set up events, and she has an event
in the pipeline – a corporate dinner with a guest speaker – but is she
being realistic about how much work is involved?

### Arthur and Mary Holleyman

This couple are unique among our contributors in having not one but
three mortgages to pay off. They were set a budget of £503 per month –
which they impressively managed to stick to.

The couple started off their money-making projects slowly, as they
spent time and energy researching speed-dating for older local residents.
Thankfully, they soon realized this idea wouldn't generate sufficient
income and turned their attention instead to re-forming Mary's small
massage therapy company, Corporate Stress Solutions (CSS). Mary decided to radically expand its client base, which meant beginning to pitch for
new work. Alongside this, she sourced high-quality dress jewellery
from the Far East, and set up Candy Crystal (CC). With launch costs
kept to a minimum, it took off and in the run-up to Christmas 2005 the
business was restricted only by its cash flow and lack of stock.

By the end of the first year, Arthur and Mary have successfully paid
off a little of what they owe, and have let their house – living elsewhere
and discovering a more simple life.

### Duncan Hume

Duncan has one of the smallest mortgages of all the contributors, yet his
lack of financial awareness and poor money-management skills suggest
that he will really struggle to pay off his £53,000 mortgage in two years.

He was set a budget of £305 per month – a budget he repeatedly failed to adhere to over the first year. But the other part of the plan was earning more money – so how did he get on? Starting his own dance troupe hit the rocks early on, but using his excellent fitness levels he started teaching a Boxercise class, earning £30 an hour.

Boxercise was the first step to making real money and the possibility arose that he could work as an agent, supplying dance and fitness instructors. Duncan's money-making then went into overdrive for a while as he taught urban ballet, offered personal training and gave Indian head massages. However, at this stage there's no way he'll pay off his mortgage in two years. As if to prove this, Duncan slipped back into his old ways and booked a holiday on which he overspent significantly. Sadly, he enters year two of the experiment looking like a sure-fire loser in the battle to pay off his mortgage early.

## Paddy and Mandy MacVean

This couple have the advantage of a relatively small mortgage – at £51,000 – but like so many others they have fallen into the trap of over-spending. They started the programme with many skills and ideas – including using Paddy's building expertise, providing dog-walking services and offering respite fostering. Their best bet seemed to be utilizing Paddy's skills to buy and do up properties to sell on for a profit. On advice he looked into buying property in Bulgaria, but after more research he decided against it. Undeterred, he investigated property closer to home and had an offer accepted on a house that needed refurbishment.

Mandy developed a prototype of a 'Birth Box', which she hopes to sell by mail order. A tailor-made time capsule that commemorates the day of a baby's birth, it includes newspapers, books and CDs and could be a real money-spinner.

They have also benefited from a little careful budgeting and economizing – shopping at a discount warehouse store and taking on an allotment and chickens. Entering the second year of the experiment, they look well on their way to making a significant dent in their mortgage.

## Dan Harding and Lucy Aldridge

Despite having opted out of the rat race, Dan and Lucy are constrained by the fetters of a £105,000 mortgage, which they would dearly love to be rid of in order to pursue their organic and environmentally sound lifestyle.

They started off the experiment well, sticking to an £88 per week budget by cutting travel and food costs. However the business side took a little longer. Dan's confidence was boosted after the Ideal Home Show where he received great advice from the show's consultant, who thought he should sell his stoves to the designer bespoke market. The UK's biggest stove-seller then met Dan and agreed to sell his stoves online for £1,200, of which Dan would get £1,000. Dan had also been making letter boxes which went down well with a conservatory company, who placed an order. He managed to complete this, but then lost motivation. Plans were delayed further when the couple decided to rent out their house and live in their shed to bring in some income.

Meanwhile, Lucy's yoga classes have received lots of interest but business is erratic. So she headed off to the Yoga Show at Olympia and got lots of interest in yoga holidays and teaching. As the first year comes to an end, Dan has finally started work again on his stoves and has managed to fulfil an order.

Dan and Lucy are driven by their desire for a free way of life rather than financial gain. They feel they would rather have a mortgage and pay it off over 35 years than lose family time. However, they are still willing to continue with the experiment.

## Heather and Chloe Wolsey-Ottaway

Heather and Chloe moved down to Cornwall from Edinburgh not long ago and would love to pay off their £90,000 mortgage.

Budgeting is something they don't find too daunting: in the first year they consistently managed to stick to their set budget of £91 per week. They sold items through local newspapers, car boot sales and auctions, raising over £4,300, but it is their business ideas that are key to making a difference.

Heather and Chloe's big idea was to make money offering a 'life laundry' decluttering service helping people reorganize their lives. They started off with some bookings, although they were briefly thrown when they discovered a rival local service. Chloe was also keen to set up a business providing entertainment for children's parties and, after investing a lot of time and money in research and promotion, they received bookings that brought in around £200 a month. Unfortunately, Chloe's enthusiasm was short-lived, as she struggled to commit to it and spend less time on her great love – painting. But selling her paintings also suffered a setback when a local exhibition failed to sell any of her work, so she then decided to focus her energies on writing. Heather too has been torn between her job and the life laundry business. As the first year ends, Heather and Chloe are trying to make some major decisions – and deciding whether that mortgage will be in Cornwall or back in Edinburgh. It will be an interesting year.

# Glossary

**Annual Percentage Rate** Also known as APR, the annual percentage rate is a measure used to compare rates of borrowing. It includes associated set-up costs and, where interest is charged more frequently, converts rates to an annual basis for ease of comparison.

**APR** (see Annual Percentage Rate)

**Accident, Sickness and Unemployment cover** An insurance policy that provides replacement income for a short period of time in the event that the policy holder is unable to work following accident, long-term illness or redundancy.

**ASU** (see Accident, Sickness and Unemployment cover)

**Bear market** A term used of stock markets to describe the situation where share prices are consistently falling over a period of time. The opposite of a Bull market.

**Blue chip company** A stock market company noted on the FTSE 100 Index, i.e., a large UK company.

**Buildings insurance** An insurance plan taken out to cover the fabric of a property. The sum assured is the full 'bricks and mortar' rebuilding cost, and may not reflect the actual market value.

**Bull Market** Market in which share prices exhibit an increasing trend for a prolonged period, hence the expression 'feeling bullish'.

**Capital assets** In mortgage terms, it is sometimes said that 'capital' is built up within a property. In this instance, the term 'capital' represents the proportion of the value of your home that is mortgage-free. Also sometimes referred to as 'equity'. When repaying 'capital' to a lender, the term refers to the repayment of a proportion of the amount originally borrowed as opposed to the interest due on the loan.

**Capital and interest mortgage** A mortgage loan with monthly repayments consisting of both the interest due on the amount borrowed and repayments of the original capital sum. Also known as a repayment mortgage.

**Capped rate** A mortgage rate with an upper ceiling beyond which it is not possible for the rate payable to rise, regardless of the level of the Bank of England base rate or the lender's standard variable mortgage rate. Often applied in conjunction with a collared rate (see below).

**Collared rate** A mortgage rate with a ceiling beyond which it is not possible for the rate payable to fall, regardless of the level of the Bank of England base rate or the lender's standard variable mortgage rate. Often applied in conjunction with a capped rate (see above).

**Compound interest** Interest paid both on the principal loan and on the interest earned during previous compounding periods. Essentially, compounding involves adding interest to the original sum and any previous interest in order to calculate interest in the next period.

**Contents insurance** Insurance that covers items that may be removed from the home, such as furniture, carpets, curtains and electrical goods. Many policies also cover personal possessions, such as jewellery. Contents cover is separate from buildings insurance, although often arranged at the same time and/or with the same provider.

**Critical illness cover** An insurance plan that pays out a guaranteed cash sum, if you are diagnosed as suffering from a specified critical illness within the term of the plan.

**Current account mortgage** A mortgage that combines your current account, personal loan, overdraft and mortgage into one account with full current account facilities (essentially a current account with a huge overdraft facility). Instead of earning interest on your savings, you pay less interest on your mortgage, with all your borrowing charged at the same rate as your mortgage.

**Discounted rate** A mortgage rate set at a level below the standard variable mortgage rate (i.e. discounted) for a set term. Redemption penalties usually apply, which in many cases extend beyond the period of the discount.

**Endowment** A policy that provides a lump sum on death or on maturity (whichever is the earlier). There are various types of endowments available, including with-profit and low-cost policies (see separate headings).

**Equity** This term is most often used as a synonym for shares (the common stock of a company, which is publicly traded on the stock market). In a mortgage context it can also refer to any proportion of the value of a property that is not mortgaged.

**Financial Services Authority (FSA)** An independent non-governmental body financed by the financial services industry and given statutory powers by the Financial Services and Markets Act 2000. The Treasury appoints the FSA Board, which establishes overall policy, but day-to-day decisions and management of the staff are the responsibility of the executive.

**Fixed rate** A mortgage rate that is guaranteed to remain fixed for a stated period, thus providing certainty to the level of your repayments. If you borrow when interest rates are high and they subsequently fall, your mortgage may look expensive. Conversely, if you borrow at a time when interest rates are low, you will continue to benefit from a fixed rate even if interest rates rise.

**Flexible mortgage** A mortgage that permits you to vary your monthly repayments. Generally, you have the option to make additional payments (overpayments) to reduce the outstanding loan more quickly, pay less without incurring penalties, or even take payment holidays. While many lenders offer this type of mortgage, it's worth noting that terms and conditions vary between providers.

***Financial Times* Stock Exchange Index of 100 Leading Shares**, or FTSE (pronounced 'footsie') 100 Index, is a figure representing the performance of the 100 largest companies listed on the London Stock Exchange. The index is seen as a barometer of success of the British economy, and is the leading share index in Europe. It is maintained by the FTSE Group, which originated as a joint venture between the *Financial Times* and the London Stock Exchange.

**Further advance** An additional loan secured against the value of your home. You may wish to take out a further advance to pay for things such as property improvement, a new car, school fees, or to invest in a private business. A further advance is sometimes referred to as a 'second mortgage'.

**Income protection insurance** An insurance policy to help you and your family maintain your current standard of living by providing long-term replacement income in the event of being unable to work due to illness or accidental injury. Income payments are usually around 60% of your current salary and commence after a predefined period.

**Index** A relative measure of value of a number of companies. For example, the FTSE 100 Index measures the aggregated, weighted value of the top 100 companies listed on the UK stock exchange.

**Individual savings account** A tax-efficient savings and investment account that allows eligible individuals to invest up to £7,000 (a maxi ISA, see below) each tax year (as at 2005/6). You can invest in either one maxi ISA or up to two mini ISAs (see below) in a tax year. Investments can be made into stocks and shares and/or cash.

**Interest** A charge for a loan, usually expressed as a percentage of the amount borrowed.

**Interest-only mortgage** A mortgage loan with monthly repayments consisting only interest due on the amount borrowed. No contributions are made towards repayment of the original capital sum, which is repayable at maturity and usually accounted for by contributions into a separate investment vehicle, such as an ISA, endowment or pension.

**ISA** (see Individual Savings Account)

**Lender** The institution (usually a bank or building society) from which funds are borrowed.

**Life cover** An arrangement designed to provide a lump sum on death. Life cover may be stand alone, such as a life assurance policy, or an integral part of a contract, such as an endowment (see above).

**Low-cost endowment** A common type of endowment (see above) with a lower sum assured than the amount of the loan. Low-cost endowments assume a rate of growth during the term that must be matched or exceeded in order to repay the loan at maturity.

**Maturity** The date on which a financial arrangement ceases. In the case of investment plans, such as endowments, it is usually the date at which proceeds become payable. For interest-only mortgages, it is the date at which the original capital must be repaid to the lender.

**Maxi ISA** A tax-efficient savings product into which £7,000 can be invested each year (as at 2005/6). All of this may be invested in stocks and shares, or up to £3,000 may be invested in cash with up to £4,000 invested in stocks and shares. It is not possible to split a maxi ISA investment between providers in a given tax year.

**Mini ISA** A tax-efficient savings product. You can invest up to £3,000 in a cash mini ISA and £4,000 into a stocks and shares mini ISA each tax year (as at 2005/06). These may be with differ-

ent providers. In practice, by investing £1 into a mini cash ISA, you limit the amount that you can invest in a stocks and shares ISA from £7,000 to £4,000.

**Monetary Policy Committee** (MPC) The Bank of England body that sets interest rates to enable the UK economy to meet the Chancellor of the Exchequer's inflation targets. The MPC is made up of nine members: the governor, two deputy governors, the bank's chief economist, the executive director for markets, and four external members appointed by the Chancellor of the Exchequer.

**Mortgage** A debt instrument in which a charge is secured against a property as collateral for the loan.

**Mortgage broker** An intermediary between two parties, normally the lender (the bank or building society) and the borrower. If you are dealing with a mortgage broker, it is important to be clear about the scope of the advice being provided and that he or she has the correct accreditation. A mortgage broker will usually advise you on the best arrangements for your circumstances and assist you in the mortgage process.

**Negative equity** A situation in which the amount of the mortgage loan exceeds the market value of the property that it is secured upon. Being in negative equity can make it difficult for a borrower to move house.

**Offset mortgage** Another term for a current account mortgage.

**Overpayments** Additional capital payments over and above those due to the lender. Overpayments are an excellent way of paying off a mortgage early.

**Payment holiday** A period during which mortgage payments are suspended. This is usually available under certain mortgage arrangements, such as offset or flexible mortgages. It is generally not advisable to take payment holidays if they can be avoided, as they serve to extend the term of the mortgage.

**Personal Equity Plan (PEP)** A tax-efficient savings plan available between 1987 and 1999, when it was replaced by the Individual Savings Account (ISA, see above). Used as a repayment vehicle to support some interest-only mortgages.

**Personal pension** An individual pension arrangement introduced in 1988 to provide lump sum and income benefits at retirement. Contributions attract income tax relief at the policyholder's highest tax rate, and build up in a favourable tax environment. Used as a vehicle to support some interest-only mortgages.

**Qualifying status** A designation given to a specific type of life policy. Suitability is governed by strict rules and stipulations, which are designed to protect the proceeds of most forms of life policies from capital gains tax or basic rate income tax.

**Redemption penalty** A charge made by the lender when all or part of a mortgage is redeemed within a stipulated period in the early years of a mortgage. Theoretically, this is to compensate the lender for the loss of business, or to recoup the benefits of a subsidized rate or cashback.

**Remortgage** An additional mortgage taken out on a home, either with the current lender or a new lender. Remortgaging is often used as an opportunity to vary the terms of the mortgage, increasing or decreasing the amount borrowed, altering the term, or switching from an interest-only to a capital and interest repayment basis. It is likely that legal costs, arrangement fees and valuation fees will be incurred.

**Repayment mortgage** A mortgage loan with monthly repayments consisting of both the interest due on the amount borrowed and repayments of the original capital sum. Also known as a capital and interest mortgage.

**Repayment vehicles** The collective term for savings plans that are used to support interest-only mortgages. The plans include endowments, Personal Equity Plans, Individual Savings Accounts and personal pensions.

**Shares** Single units of ownership in a corporation, often represented by a stock certificate. The price is determined by supply and demand.

**Standard variable rate**
The mortgage lender's main mortgage interest rate, which usually fluctuates with changes in the Bank of England base rate.

**Stock market** An exchange where stocks, bonds or other securities are bought and sold.

**Stocks** Fixed-interest securities, such as gilts (Treasury stock). They are traded on stock exchanges, where their prices fluctuate according to demand and other influencing factors, including interest rates and time to redemption.

**SWOT analysis** A tool for auditing an organization and its environment. It is the first stage of planning and helps focus on key issues. SWOT stands for Strengths and Weaknesses (which are internal factors), Opportunities and Threats (which are external factors).

**Tax Exempt Special Savings Account** Better known as TESSAs, these were set up in 1991 and allowed individuals to invest a maximum of £9,000 over five years into a special savings account run by a bank or building society. Provided the money was left in the account for the whole five years, it could be withdrawn at the end of the term completely free of tax. TESSAs were replaced in 1999 by ISAs (see above).

**TESSA** (see Tax Exempt Special Savings Account)

**Tracker mortgage** A variable-rate mortgage in which the interest tracks or follows an index, usually the Bank of England's base rate. This means that your monthly repayments alter in accordance with changes in the index (usually after a period of, say, 14 days).

**Variable rate** Also known as standard variable rate (see above).

**With-profit endowment** A type of endowment contract that is invested in the with-profit fund of an insurance company. With-profit funds are designed to smooth out the fluctuations normally associated with stock market investments, but have varying degrees of success.

# Useful Websites

**Association of British Insurers**
The ABI (Association of British Insurers) represents the collective interests of the UK's insurance industry, often speaking out and issuing guidance on issues of common interest.
www.abi.org.uk

**Association of Policy Market Makers**
Useful information on companies that buy and sell with-profit endowment policies. APMM and all its members are regulated under the Financial Services Authority.
www.apmm.org

**AWD plc**
One of the UK's largest independent financial advisers, with 24 offices and over 300 professional advisers.
www.awdplc.com

**Bank of England**
The Bank of England sets interest rates in the UK to manage inflation and maintains the banking system, including the issue of banknotes. Monthly minutes of the Monetary Policy Committee are available on this site.
www.bankofengland.co.uk

**BBC**
A wide range of advice: from foreign languages to finance.
www.bbc.co.uk

**British Franchise Association**
A source of information on franchises and franchise opportunities in the UK.
www.british-franchise.org
or tel. 01491 578050

**Business Link**
Business Link is an easy-to-use business support, advice and information service managed by the DTI.
www.businesslink.gov.uk
or tel. 0845 600 9 006

**Camping and Caravanning Club**
Useful advice for anyone considering a camping holiday – from beginner to veteran.
www.campingandcaravanning club.co.uk

**Council of Mortgage Lenders**
A trade association representing 98% of the UK residential lending industry. This useful website contains a wide selection of publications, press releases and statistics.
www.cml.org.uk

**Financial Services Authority**
The financial services regulator and watchdog in the UK. The FSA is an independent body with a wide range of rule-making, investigatory and enforcement powers. Its responsibilities include consumer protection and it is answerable to the Government.
www.fsa.gov.uk

## Moneyextra

An award-winning website with comparisons of mortgages, loans, credit cards and much more.
www.moneyextra.co.uk

## National Cycle Network

A useful site for cyclists. It also contains an online map of the network which can be searched using your postcode or town name.
www.nationalcyclenetwork.org.uk

## National Savings

National Savings is backed by HM Treasury and offers financial products – many of which are 100% guaranteed. It is also the home of premium bonds and includes a facility whereby you can check past draws to see if your numbers have come up.
www.nsandi.com

## NHS Smoking Helpline

An online resource for everything you need to stop smoking and stay stopped. For more help and advice call the NHS smoking helpline on 0800 169 0 169 or visit
www.givingupsmoking.co.uk

## National Society of Allotment and Leisure Gardeners

A useful site with information to help all enjoy the recreation of gardening and so promote health, education and community fellowship.
www.nsalg.org.uk

## Prince's Trust

A UK charity that offers practical support including training, mentoring and financial assistance, to help 14–30 year olds realize their potential and transform their lives.
www.princes-trust.org.uk

## Relate

Relate offers advice, relationship counselling, workshops, mediation, consultations and support face-to-face, by phone or through the website.
www.relate.org.uk

## Shopping comparisons

A leading shopping search engine which searches thousands of Internet sites to find the cheapest place to purchase almost anything.
www.kelkoo.co.uk

## Sustainable Transport Charity

Sustrans is the UK's leading sustainable transport charity, working on practical projects so people can choose to travel in ways that benefit their health and their environment.
www.sustrans.co.uk

# Appendix

## 21 STEPS TO MORTGAGE HEAVEN

**1.** Work out how much interest you have to pay over the term – don't just focus on the basic loan. The total sum will probably be frightening enough to galvanize you into action.

**2.** Find out if you have an interest-only or repayment mortgage. If interest-only, have you considered how you are going to pay off the actual capital element of your mortgage?

**3.** If you have an endowment, don't rely on it to pay off your mortgage. Check how much it's worth now and what it is likely to be worth at maturity. Don't forget that you'll have to pay for any shortfall. You might want to switch to a capital repayment mortgage.

**4.** Your monthly mortgage repayments may appear relatively small and manageable, but work out how much you are paying annually and express it as a percentage of your annual income. When the amount is expressed annually and in thousands of pounds as a percentage of your annual income, it is likely to focus your mind on repaying it sooner rather than later. The benefit in terms of interest payments saved can be huge.

**5.** Don't assume that property prices always go up. They don't. Ask anyone who got caught out by falling property prices and higher interest rates in the late 1980s. The overt bullishness surrounding current property prices may not be sustainable and should make you more cautious. If in doubt, don't borrow more than you can foreseeably afford, and fix your mortgage rate to be safe rather than sorry.

**6.** As a general rule, pay off your debt – whether it be a personal loan, credit card bill or mortgage – as soon as you can, and certainly before you consider investing in the stock market. The certainty of paying off debt is more sensible than the uncertainty of the stock market.

**7.** Be vigilant about the interest rates applying to your personal loans and credit cards, as well as those on your mortgage. Visiting an online broking organization to compare figures could save you several thousand pounds in interest charges.

**8.** Go for interest-free offers on credit cards whenever you can, but don't forget to recheck when the interest-free period has finished.

**9.** Regularly check your mortgage rate against the best offers available. These can be found in the national press or on TV programmes, such as BBC2's *Working Lunch*.

**10.** Think about your mortgage in the context of your overall financial position, age, lifestyle, pension requirements and the amount of risk you can take. For example, if you are fairly certain of receiving a sizeable inheritance from a relative at some stage, you might feel more comfortable about taking on a larger mortgage. Never forget that you are going to have to pay off your mortgage at some point.

**11.** Don't forget that there are several costs involved in buying and selling houses. These include Stamp Duty, solicitor's fees, surveyor's fees, life cover, house insurance and income protection, as well as the cost of arranging a mortgage.

**12.** Go for a reputable mortgage broker who can offer you the very best mortgage from the whole of the market, and who operates on a fee-free basis. Moneyextra Mortgages Ltd (www.moneyextra.com) is one of the very few to do this.

**13.** If you arranged your personal mortgage protection policies, such as life cover and income protection, some years ago, it is often worthwhile rebroking them, as protection rates have eased in your favour in recent years and you may well get a cheaper option.

**14.** Don't forget to compare quotes for your household general insurance rates every year. Rates between companies can vary hugely, so don't take the lazy option and do nothing: it will almost certainly cost you money – sometimes a substantial amount. As soon as the renewal reminder pops through the letter box, start your research.

**15.** If you have never owned property before, you will need to allow a regular amount for upkeep. Some things, such as plumbing, wiring and tiles falling off the roof, are often not covered by insurance. If possible, keep an easy access cash account with some money in it for these unforeseeable events. Try not to go overdrawn, as it will often add disproportionately to your costs.

**16.** It's very easy to slip into the debt trap – especially when loans and credit are so widely available. Don't forget that it's much easier to slip into debt than it is to get out of it.

**17.** As my old mum used to say, when you are spending money, first spend cash, then use a cheque and after that a credit card. Psychologically, most of us find it much more difficult to spend cash than writing a cheque or using a credit card. It's almost as if the perceived value of cash is greater than a sum spent on a credit card – even though the amount may be exactly the same.

**18.** Cut up your credit cards.

**19.** Budgeting can solve up to half the problem of how to pay off your mortgage early. Make a reasonable and realistic budget and stick to it. Keep in mind that you won't have to do it for ever. Once you have paid off your mortgage, the lessons you have learnt about budgeting should stay with you for ever and make you more aware of how you spend money in the future.

**20.** If you are trying to keep to a weekly food budget, take out the relevant amount in cash at the beginning of the week and use only that to purchase your food.

**21.** Above all, remember that you're not paying off your mortgage for its own sake. It's about giving yourself choices about your future and how you can lead the rest of your life.

# Index